Jossey-Bass Teac

Jossey-Bass Teacher provides educators with practical knowledge and tools to create a positive and lifelong impact on student learning. We offer classroom-tested and research-based teaching resources for a variety of grade levels and subject areas. Whether you are an aspiring, new, or veteran teacher, we want to help you make every teaching day your best.

From ready-to-use classroom activities to the latest teaching framework, our value-packed books provide insightful, practical, and comprehensive materials on the topics that matter most to K–12 teachers. We hope to become your trusted source for the best ideas from the most experienced and respected experts in the field.

The Teacher's Big Book of Graphic Organizers

100 Reproducible Organizers That Help Kids with Reading, Writing, and the Content Areas

KATHERINE S. McKNIGHT

JOSSEY-BASS
A Wiley Imprint
www.josseybass.com

CONTENTS

Chapter Four Graphic Organizers for Note Taking and Study Skills 75

Chapter Five Graphic Organizers for Supporting Reading Comprehension 115

Chapter Six   Graphic Organizers for Writing   163

ACKNOWLEDGMENTS

My journey as an educator began when I was a high school teacher more than twenty years ago. Early on, I knew that best teaching practices were central to successful classroom teaching and learning. I would try anything. Beverly LaCoste, a wonderful educator and my principal for several years, proclaimed, "Katie Mac, I can send you to a conference, and the next day you're trying something new." It's true. I'm a tinkerer. Always looking for another instructional strategy or another idea, I motivate my students who are preparing to become middle school and high school teachers to be eclectic and work to reach all kinds of learners. And eclectic teaching and reaching all types of learners are really what this book is about. The more strategies we employ, the more likely we are to succeed in reaching *all* our students.

There are many individuals whom I wish to thank who have supported my efforts to make this book a valuable teaching resource. Ellie McKnight, Celia Woldt, Laura Woldt, Olivia Doe, and Sydney Lawson were instrumental in making the student samples feature a success. My graduate assistant, Astrid Rodrigues, is always patient and diligent. My husband, Jim, is always supportive of my work and often reminds me that teaching is my vocation. Colin, my son, is a constant reminder that even when our work is challenging, we educators must remember that all children are beautifully different. I also want to thank my sister, Mary (a writing teacher), who often helped me get back on the horse when I fell off. I am grateful to the supportive staff at Jossey-Bass. It is a joy to work with an editor like Margie McAneny. Justin Frahm's attention to detail and artistic finesse were critical to the design of this book. Finally, I must acknowledge my first teacher and mentor, my mom, Patricia Siewert (1934–2008). Mom was a teacher in the Chicago public schools for more than thirty-four years; she taught me that teaching was truly an act of love and social justice. I often sought teaching advice from her, and she was, and will always be, my "BFF."

For Jim, Ellie, and Colin, who bring joy to my life

ABOUT THE AUTHOR

Katherine S. McKnight, Ph.D., has been a literacy educator for over twenty years. A former high school English teacher, she currently works as an associate professor of secondary education at National-Louis University. She also trains educators regularly as a professional development consultant for the National Council of Teachers of English. Katie publishes regularly in professional journals and is a frequent presenter at education conferences. She has coauthored numerous books for teachers, including *Teaching Writing in the Inclusive Classroom* (with Roger Passman; Jossey-Bass, 2007), *Teaching the Classics in the Inclusive Classroom* (with Bradley Berlage; Jossey-Bass, 2007), *The Second City Guide to Improv in the Classroom* (with Mary Scruggs; Jossey-Bass, 2008), and *Teaching English in Middle and Secondary Schools, 5th Edition* (with Rhoda Maxwell and Mary Meiser; Pearson, 2010). Katie lives in Chicago with her husband and children.

CHAPTER ONE

Why Are Graphic Organizers Such Important Tools for Teaching and Learning?

Graphic organizers are important and effective pedagogical tools for organizing content and ideas and facilitating learners' comprehension of newly acquired information. Gardner's theory of multiple intelligences (1993, 2006) posits that students are better able to learn and internalize information when more than one learning modality is employed in an instructional strategy. Because graphic organizers present material through the visual and spatial modalities (and reinforce what is taught in the classroom), the use of graphic organizers helps students internalize what they are learning.

For today's classroom, nothing is more essential to successful teaching and learning than strategy-based instruction. It is through the use of specific teaching strategies and learning tools that students can be more successful learners. Graphic organizers are teaching and learning tools; when they're integrated into classroom experiences, students are better able to understand new material. Creating a strong visual picture, graphic organizers support students by enabling them to literally see connections and relationships between facts, information, and terms.

This book contains 100 graphic organizers, teaching and learning tools that support success and active, effective learning in the classroom. Students are prompted to ask questions and encouraged to build and apply crucial thinking skills while developing tools for learning. You can use the graphic organizers in this book for

- Curriculum planning and development
- Teaching and supporting student comprehension in learning new material
- Classroom assessment
- Building students' learning skills

Reaching *All* Learners

By integrating text and visual imagery, the 100 graphic organizers featured in this book actively engage a wide variety of learners, including students with special needs and English language learners. These organizers can be used for any subject matter and are easily integrated into course curriculum.

We know from learning theory that the human mind naturally organizes and stores information. Our minds create structures to store newly acquired information and connect it to previous knowledge (Piaget, 1974). The graphic organizers featured in this book are visualizations of these mental storage systems, and serve to support students in remembering and connecting information (Vygotsky, 1962). When students are able to remember and assimilate information, they can delve into more critical thinking.

Numerous studies have found graphic organizers to be effective for teaching and learning, and many support the effectiveness of graphic organizers for gifted children and students with special needs (Cassidy, 1991). Textbook publishers have taken note of the research that supports the importance of graphic organizers for teaching and learning, and regularly feature them in textbooks.

Because graphic organizers are widely successful, these learning tools are used at all grade levels. They are also effective for adult learners. Community colleges and corporate entities use graphic organizers to present information in similar instructive contexts. Often you will see college-level textbooks and corporate instructional materials use graphic organizers. The visually stimulating nature of graphic organizers draws the learner's attention. As learners, we attend to what is novel and visually intriguing because the brain is more equipped to process images than text. Because graphic organizers integrate text and visual images, learners are having more whole-brain experiences.

In addition, for all learners, but for adult learners in particular, graphic organizers facilitate the integration of long-term memory and new learning. Adult learners generally have more background and long-term knowledge, and graphic organizers bridge what adult learners already know with what they are learning. Graphic organizers actually trigger long-term memory and promote synthesis with new information (Materna, 2007).

Getting Started

This book is divided into chapters based on the different applications of the graphic organizers. You, the teacher, are the best judge of which organizers are best for a given lesson. Here are some suggestions and bits of advice as you decide which organizers to use for a specific instructional purpose:

Modeling. It is critical to model the graphic organizer when you present it to the class. Show the students how you, as a learner, use this organizer to understand material.

Learning experiences. You can use the graphic organizers in this book for individual or small group instruction. In general, graphic organizers are great for cooperative learning because they provide a structure for the students.

Assessment. Assessment should be reliable and varied. As students progress through middle school and high school, quizzes and tests become more common, but they are only one kind of assessment. Graphic organizers can be easily used for classroom assessment. For example, you could use the Questioning the Author activity (Chapter Five) to determine if the students read the pages that were assigned for homework. You will probably gain greater insight into the students' comprehension of the text than you would with a multiple-choice reading quiz.

Special needs. Students with special needs often have difficulty decoding and comprehending text and developing vocabulary. This makes reading even more challenging. Here are some suggestions to support students with special needs when they use the graphic organizers in this book:

1. Physically divide some of the organizers by cutting, folding, or highlighting different sections. This helps the students focus on one section and activity at a time.
2. Use a highlighter or different colors for the graphic organizer headings to help students process and focus on key information.
3. Have students work in pairs or in small groups, as needed. Students who have difficulty with attention and reading will benefit from working with their peers. Working in a social setting helps all students work collaboratively and take responsibility for their own learning. We want our students to develop self-efficacy in their learning experiences.
4. Create reading frames for students. Using heavy card stock or cardboard, create frames of different sizes so that students can place them over sections. This helps students focus on one section at a time.
5. Encourage students to use vocabulary logs or notebooks. All the vocabulary graphic organizers that are featured in Chapter Three can be used as templates for a vocabulary log or notebook. This is a student-created vocabulary reference book to which the students can refer during the course of the school year.

Variations. There is no one right way to visually represent information. Your students may have several variations of the same organizer for a given topic or subject. Further, some students are more visually oriented than others, so you should expect to see a range of results. Particularly helpful to English language learners, the graphic organizers featured in this book support students in understanding language more easily with the assistance of visual images.

The key to successful teaching and learning is to employ a wide variety of strategies. I hope that the 100 graphic organizers in this book will add to your repertoire of strategies to reach *all* kinds of learners in your teaching.

You can download PDF versions of the graphic organizers found in this book at
www.josseybass.com/go/graphicorganizers
Password: 4g6hn7

CHAPTER TWO
Graphic Organizers for Brainstorming and Idea Generation

1 Power Thinking (Levels of Brainstorming)

▶ Grades 6–12
▶ Social studies, English, science, health

Power Thinking is a graphic organizer that allows learners to organize ideas and information hierarchically. As an alternative form of outlining, this tool can be used to group terms, ideas, and vocabulary, for example, into main headings and subheadings.

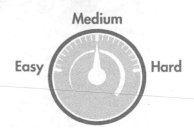

Tips for Classroom Implementation

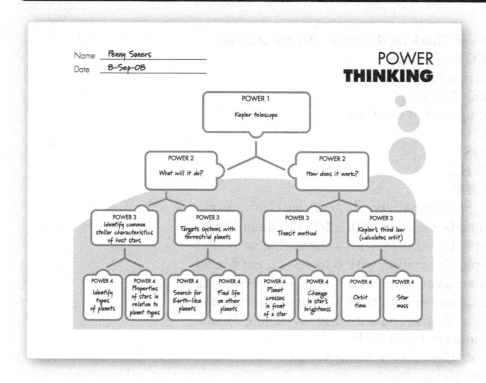

When this graphic organizer is implemented into instruction, it is acceptable for the students to add information at the different levels. If there are more than two ideas or details at power 2 that support the identified main idea in power 1, this is fine. The students need to understand that the Power Thinking template is malleable. As teachers we need to place greater emphasis on the students' thinking and their ability to organize information in a hierarchy rather than on completing the template as it is exactly presented.

Another important consideration for power thinking is the notion that there is more than one way to organize information Individual thinking always varies. Instead of emphasizing one particular answer, we need to focus on the *process* of thinking in arranging, organizing, and representing information.

When the students work on the Power Thinking organizer, I like to have them in groups of three students or in pairs. As we progress through the different levels of the organizer, the students can discuss points of information or details to include. This approach naturally shifts the focus: this becomes less a teacher-directed activity and more of a student-directed activity in which you take on the role of facilitator.

POWER THINKING

Name _____

Date _____

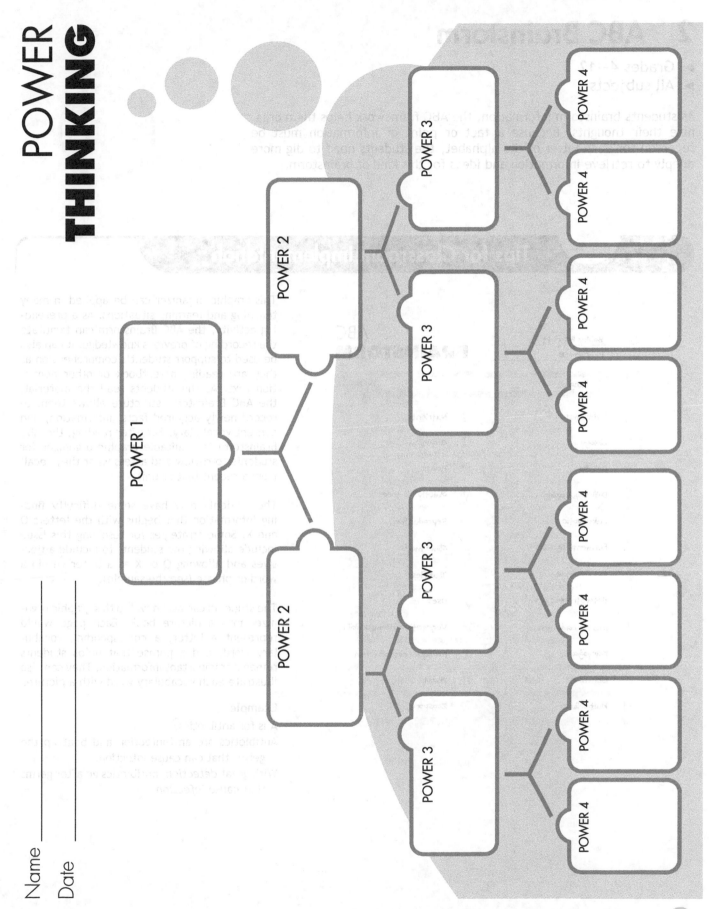

| POWER 1 |

| POWER 2 | POWER 2 |

| POWER 3 | POWER 3 | POWER 3 | POWER 3 |

| POWER 4 | POWER 4 | POWER 4 | POWER 4 | POWER 4 | POWER 4 | POWER 4 | POWER 4 |

2 ABC Brainstorm

► Grades 4–12
► All subjects

As students brainstorm information, the ABC framework helps them organize their thoughts. Because a fact or point of information must be recorded for each letter of the alphabet, the students need to dig more deeply to retrieve information and ideas for this kind of brainstorm.

Tips for Classroom Implementation

Name   Bobby Barrett
Date   10–Sep–08

ABC BRAINSTORM

Topic   Fungus

A	Antibiotics		N	Nutrients
B	Biology		O	Organism
C	Cellulose		P	Plants
D	DNA sequencing		Q	Quietly kill trees
E	Eukaryotic		R	Reproduction
F	Fermentation		S	Slime molds
G	Green algae		T	Truffles
H	Heterotrophic		U	Uses
I	Ionizing radiation		V	Vegetative incompatibility
K	Karyogamy		X	Ase(x)ual reproduction
L	Lichens		Y	Yeasts
M	Multicellular		Z	Zoospore

This graphic organizer can be applied in many teaching and learning situations. As a prereading activity, the ABC Brainstorm can facilitate the recording of previous knowledge. It can also be used to support student's comprehension as they are reading a textbook or other nonfiction text. As the students read the material, the ABC Brainstorm structure allows them to record newly acquired facts, information, and content vocabulary. For after reading, the ABC Brainstorm is a suitable graphic organizer for students to review and assess what they recall from a recent text or unit.

The students may have some difficulty finding information that begins with the letters Q and X. Some strategies for resolving this issue include allowing the students to include adjectives and allowing Q or X as a letter within a word or phrase (see the sample).

The students can also develop this graphic organizer into a picture book. Each page would represent a letter, a corresponding vocabulary word, and a phrase that helps students remember important information. They can also illustrate each vocabulary word with a picture.

Example
A is for antibiotics.
Antibiotics are anti-infection and beat up the germs that can cause infection.
With great *detection,* antibiotics go after germs that cause *infection.*

Name _____

Date _____

ABC
BRAINSTORM

Topic		

A		N	
B		O	
C		P	
D		Q	
E		R	
F		S	
G		T	
H		U	
I		V	
K		X	
L		Y	
M		Z	

3 Carousel Brainstorm

▶ Grades 4–12
▶ All subjects

Whether the students are activating prior knowledge or reviewing newly acquired information, this organizer allows them to identify and study subtopics within a larger topic.

Tips for Classroom Implementation

Name _Anisha Bryant_

Date _20-Nov-08_

CAROUSEL BRAINSTORM

Here is a sample of a carousel brainstorm for *Diary of a Wimpy Kid*. Each box represents a sheet of large chart paper.

What do you know about the author?

The author is Jeff Kinney.

He develops video games.

He has a website www.wimpykid.com

He wrote two more Wimpy Kid books.

What do you know about the main character?

His name is Greg Heffley.

He's in middle school.

His mom makes him keep a diary.

He has 2 brothers.

List as many things as you can about the setting of the book.

There are a bunch of settings in the book.

Halloween in the neighborhood.

Greg lives in a house.

He can walk to his friend's house.

It seems like a nice place.

What happens in the book? What are the "key events"?

Greg and his best friend Rowley have a big fight.

Greg lies and gets his best friend in trouble.

Greg and Rowley become best friends at the end.

Write down some descriptions that you "liked."

P. 134 The spider.

PP. 126-128 Christmas present.

P. 131 Big wheel going down the hill.

PP. 100-101 School play.

What questions do you have about the book so far?

Since Greg and Rowley became friends again, will Greg treat Rowley better?

What will they do in the summer?

Divide the students into groups of three or four. Identify subtopics and write each one on a separate sheet of large paper. In each group, a student will serve as the recorder, using an assigned colored marker, which makes it easy to associate each group with its comments. Explain to the students that they will have a brief time, about thirty to forty-five seconds, to write down everything they can think of for each topic. The different sheets with the different topics will be passed to each group. As the sheets progress through the groups, it will be necessary to extend the time allowed for each sheet because the students will have to read what has already been recorded by the other groups, and they will probably find it more challenging to add new information. The carousel is complete when the students have their original sheet.

Students often compare this exercise to electronic blogging. They enjoy reading, responding to, and adding to each others' comments and ideas. As the students engage in this activity in the classroom, there is often discussion as they progress from one chart to another.

When I have used this activity in the classroom, I allow (and sometimes encourage) the students to use language taken directly from the text. When students closely examine text, they are actively analyzing what they are reading.

Name _____

Date _____

Each box represents a sheet of large chart paper.

What do you know about the author?

What do you know about the main character?

List as many things as you can about the setting of the book.

What happens in the book? What are the "key events"?

Write down some descriptions that you "liked."

What questions do you have about the book so far?

4 Venn Diagram

▶ Grades 4—12
▶ All subjects

Venn diagrams are graphic organizers that provide a visual comparison of similarities and differences between subjects. The structure of this organizer is applicable to a wide variety of topics.

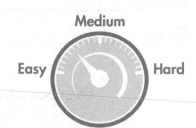

Tips for Classroom Implementation

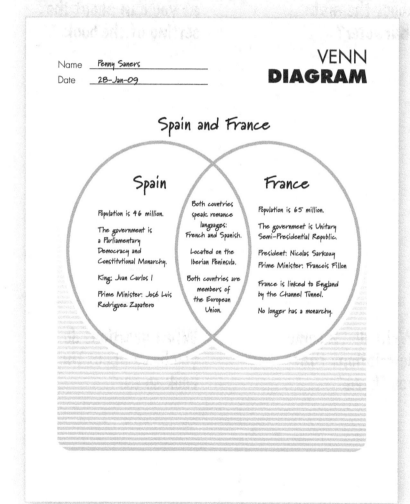

Name   Penny Saners
Date   28-Jan-09

VENN
DIAGRAM

Spain and France

Spain

Population is 46 million.

The government is a Parliamentary Democracy and Constitutional Monarchy.

King: Juan Carlos I

Prime Minister: José Luis Rodriguez Zapatero

Both countries speak romance languages: French and Spanish.

Located on the Iberian Peninsula.

Both countries are members of the European Union.

France

Population is 65 million.

The government is Unitary Semi-Presidential Republic.

President: Nicolas Sarkozy
Prime Minister: Francois Fillon

France is linked to England by the Channel Tunnel.

No longer has a monarchy.

Venn diagrams can be easily adapted to include more than two topics and one common area. Once the students have completed the Venn diagram, they should discuss and explain what they have included in the circles and common area(s). These discussions can be completed in large or small group discussions.

The middle area where the two circles overlap can be tricky. Sometimes the students become confused and continue to put opposites or comparisons in this space. Using different colored markers or pencils for each circle and the overlapping intersection is a simple adaptation that allows students to see the differences and similarities in the presented information from the onset.

Name _____

Date _____

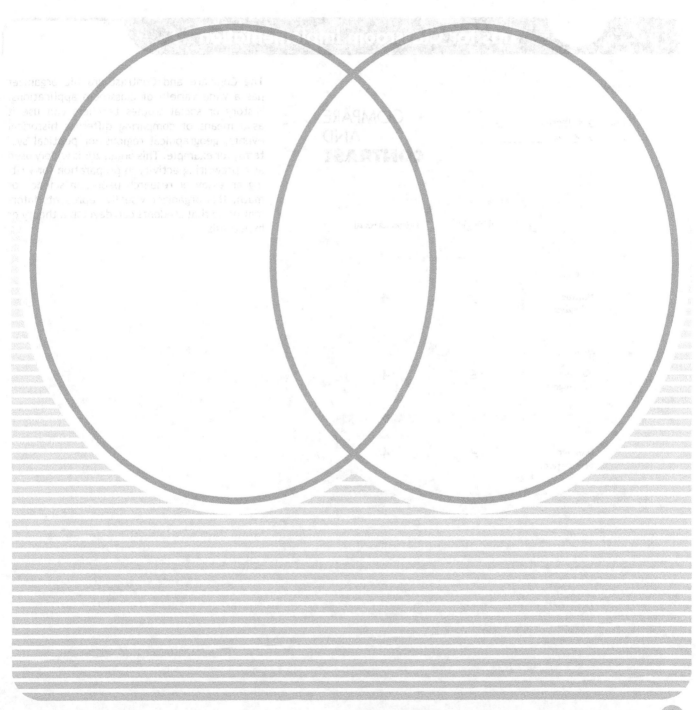

5 Compare and Contrast

▶ Grades 4–12
▶ All subjects

This graphic organizer is useful for looking at two items and figuring out the similarities and differences between them. The students should look first for the similarities and then the differences.

Tips for Classroom Implementation

Name _Bobby Barrett_
Date _24-Sep-08_

COMPARE
AND
CONTRAST

	Name 1 Triangle	Name 2 Quadrilateral
Attribute 1 Number of sides	3	4
Attribute 2 Number of angles	3	4
Attribute 3 Number of vertices	3	4

The Compare and Contrast graphic organizer has a wide variety of classroom applications. History or social studies teachers can use it as a means of comparing different historical events, geographical regions, or political systems, for example. This organizer is widely used as a prewriting activity in preparation for writing an essay or research paper. In science or math, this organizer visually represents information so that students can develop a theory or hypothesis.

Name _____

Date _____

COMPARE AND **CONTRAST**

	Name 1	**Name 2**
Attribute 1		
Attribute 2		
Attribute 3		

6 KWL

▶ Grades 6–12
▶ All subjects, but particularly useful as a preview for a new unit or a prereading activity

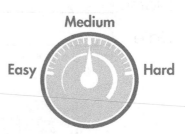

Created by Donna Ogle, the KWL strategy is a three-column chart that captures the before, during, and after stages of reading.

K = What a reader already *knows* about the selected text topic. Students tap into their prior knowledge before they begin reading. As we know from research in reading, prior knowledge supports student comprehension.

W = What a student *wants* to know about the selected text topic. Students' asking questions before they read a text also supports their comprehension.

L = What the students *learned* about the topic. Students' reflecting and thinking about what they just read aids them in their ability to synthesize newly acquired information with prior knowledge.

Tips for Classroom Implementation

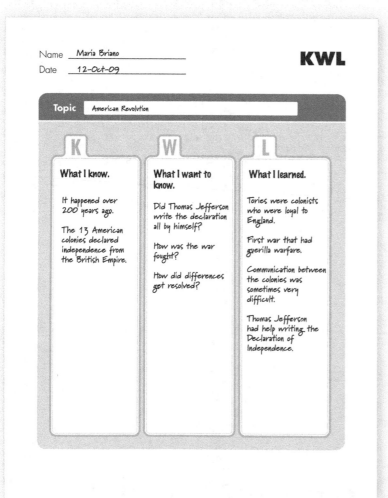

Often used at the beginning of an instructional unit, the KWL strategy is one of the most widely recognized graphic organizers and instructional strategies. It can be used for individual, small-group, and large-group instruction. There is significant evidence that when learners tap into previous knowledge and pose individual questions, they are more likely to become engaged in their learning and more apt to internalize what they learn.

To support all kinds of learners, consider using different colors for each column. The students may also draw or visually represent their knowledge and ideas for each column.

Name _____

Date _____

Topic _____

K
What I know.

W
What I want to know.

L
What I learned.

7 KWS

► Grades 4—12
► All subjects—particularly useful for a Web search or as an introduction to an I search or research paper

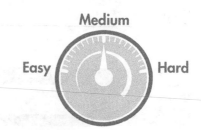

The KWS organizer is a modified KWL that incorporates sources for researching the topic and question.

Tips for Classroom Implementation

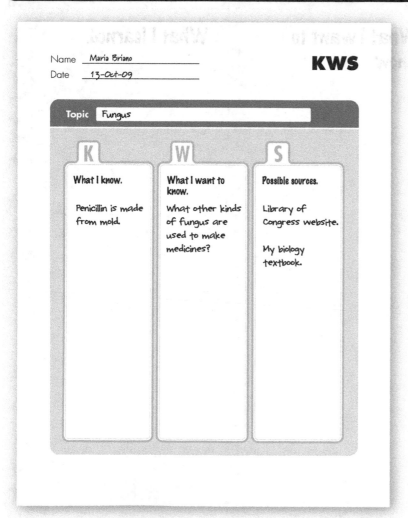

Name Maria Briano

Date 13-Oct-09

KWS

Topic Fungus

K
What I know.

Penicillin is made from mold.

W
What I want to know.

What other kinds of fungus are used to make medicines?

S
Possible sources.

Library of Congress website.

My biology textbook.

Obtaining access to sources for research in the classroom is helpful for the students as they answer posed questions. Once the students complete the S (Possible Sources) column, they can convert the information and sources they found into a bibliography following MLA, APA, or other formatting.

At a time when students are inundated with information from media resources, they need a systematic strategy to organize, understand, and synthesize. The KWS is one strategy that students can use to organize information.

Name _____

Date _____

Topic [   ]

K

What I know.

W

What I want to know.

S

Possible sources.

8 KWHL

► Grades 9—12
► Social studies

KWHL is a modified KWL that incorporates primary and secondary resources for research. Students are able to incorporate prior knowledge as they create a plan for investigating a topic.

K = What do I already *know*?
W = What do I *want* to find out?
H = *How* am I going to find out?
L = What did I *learn*?

Tips for Classroom Implementation

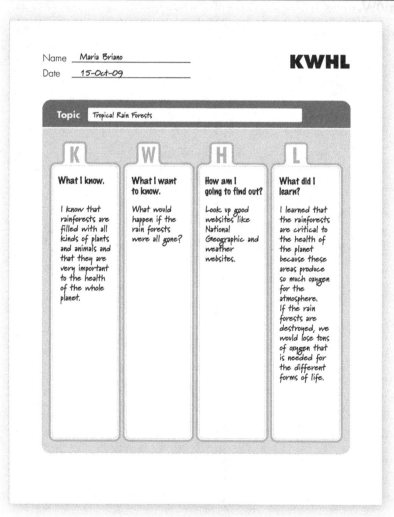

Accessibility to primary and secondary sources is necessary for the students to answer posed questions. When I ask students to pose their own questions, I often find that they are confused and hesitant because they fear that they will ask the "wrong" question or simply aren't sure where to begin. This organizer is especially useful for students who are posing their own questions through Web searches or are engaged in inquiry projects.

Name _____

Date _____

KWHL

Topic [   ]

K	W	H	L
What I know.	**What I want to know.**	**How am I going to find out?**	**What did I learn?**

9 KWLT

▶ Grades 4–12
▶ All subjects

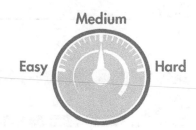

KWLT is modeled after the KWL strategy. In this version, students are prompted to engage in the metacognitive experience of talking to peers about what they have learned and teaching the material to others.

K = What do I already *know*?
W = What do I *want* to find out?
L = What did I *learn*?
T = What do I want to *tell* others?

Tips for Classroom Implementation

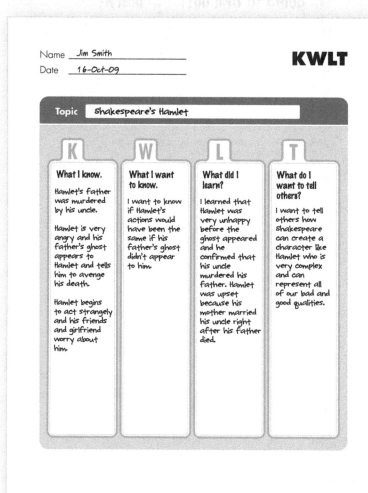

Name Jim Smith
Date 16-Oct-09

KWLT

Topic Shakespeare's Hamlet

K

What I know.

Hamlet's father was murdered by his uncle.

Hamlet is very angry and his father's ghost appears to Hamlet and tells him to avenge his death.

Hamlet begins to act strangely and his friends and girlfriend worry about him.

W

What I want to know.

I want to know if Hamlet's actions would have been the same if his father's ghost didn't appear to him.

L

What did I learn?

I learned that Hamlet was very unhappy before the ghost appeared and he confirmed that his uncle murdered his father. Hamlet was upset because his mother married his uncle right after his father died.

T

What do I want to tell others?

I want to tell others how Shakespeare can create a character like Hamlet who is very complex and can represent all of our bad and good qualities.

For the T column of this graphic organizer, the students can teach in pairs, or the class can participate in a cooperative learning activity, such as a jigsaw.

KWLT, the final variation of KWL, contains a reflective component. As in the foundational KWL experiences, the students

1. brainstorm what they already know about a topic
2. pose questions about what they want to learn
3. reflect on what they learned
4. The ''T'', the last step for the KWLT strategy, prompts students to teach what they have learned.

It is through the last step in this teaching and learning strategy that students are more able to internalize the information that they have learned, since they are now practicing their understanding for the new material through teaching it.

Name _____

Date _____

KWLT

Topic	

K — What I know.

W — What I want to know.

L — What did I learn?

T — What do I want to tell others?

10 Topic Generation with 3 Ideas–Linear Model

▶ Grades 4–12
▶ All subjects

Tips for Classroom Implementation

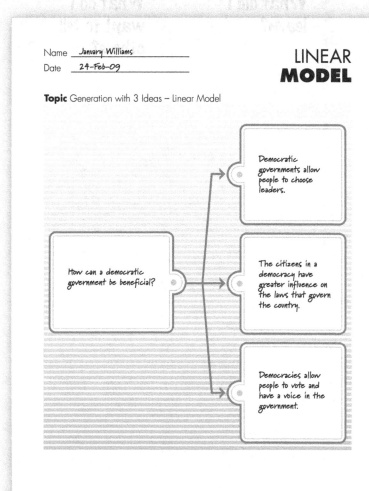

Name __Janvary Williams__
Date __24-Feb-09__

LINEAR MODEL

Topic Generation with 3 Ideas – Linear Model

How can a democratic government be beneficial?

Democratic governments allow people to choose leaders.

The citizens in a democracy have greater influence on the laws that govern the country.

Democracies allow people to vote and have a voice in the government.

It is always helpful to model graphic organizers before the students apply them on their own. As the teacher, you can model how these graphic organizers are used to document and generate topics and ideas.

Remind students that it is always useful to adapt these graphic organizers as needed. The emphasis should not be on filling out all squares or circles. Instead, students should use these topic generation graphic organizers so that they can begin to observe

• connections between new material and
• prior learning
• patterns and main ideas
• relationships between key ideas

Graphic organizers 10 through 17 offer students the opportunity to visualize and organize their ideas. They have a wide variety of applications, the most common of which are for essay or research paper topic organization and other writing activities.

Name _____

Date _____

Topic Generation with 3 Ideas – Linear Model

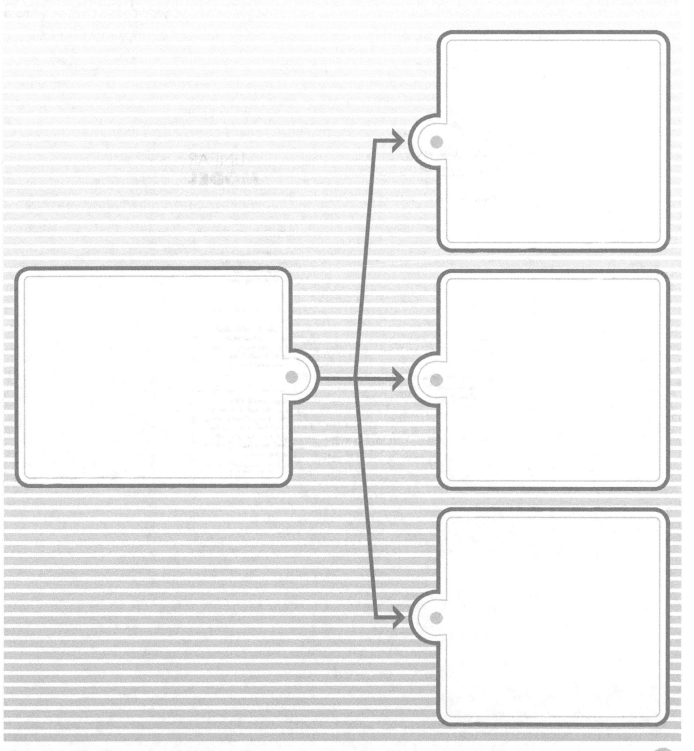

11 Topic Generation with 4 Ideas–Linear Model

▶ Grades 4–12
▶ All subjects

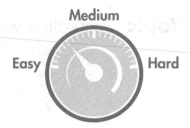

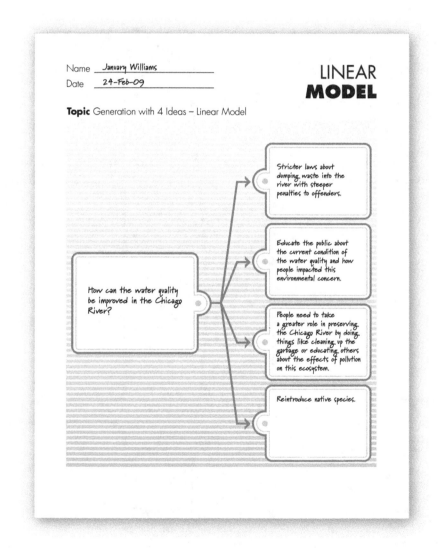

Name _____

Date _____

Topic Generation with 4 Ideas – Linear Model

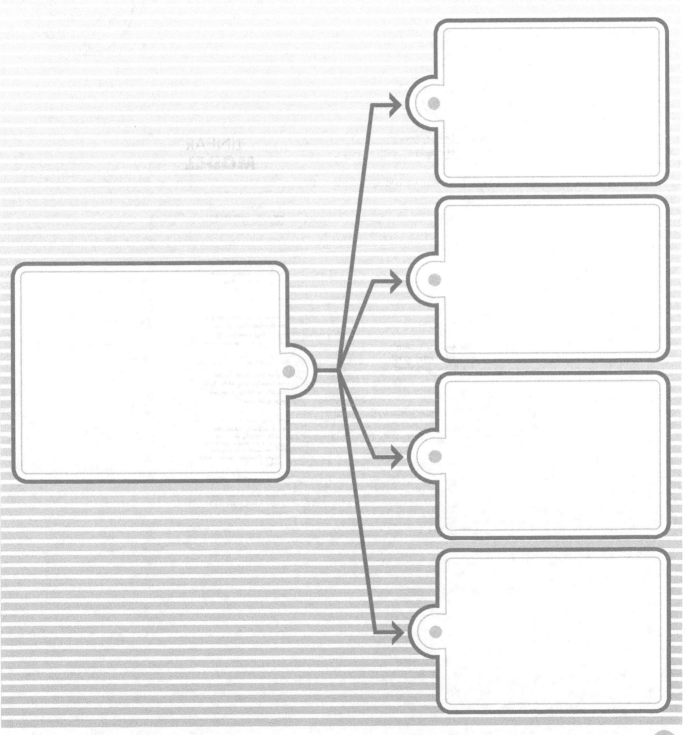

12 Topic Generation with 6 Ideas–Linear Model

▶ Grades 4–12
▶ All subjects

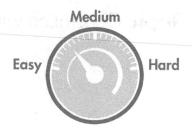

Easy — Medium — Hard

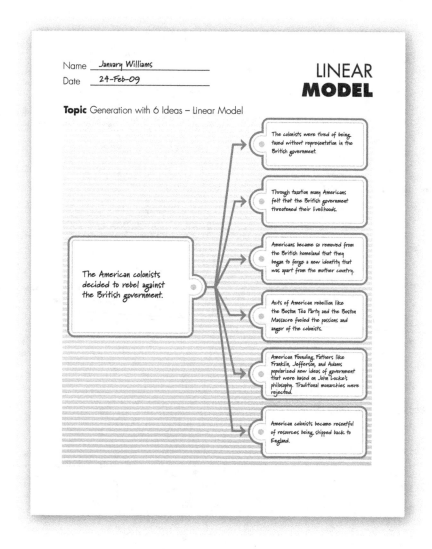

Name   January Williams
Date   24-Feb-09

LINEAR
MODEL

Topic Generation with 6 Ideas – Linear Model

The American colonists decided to rebel against the British government.

- The colonists were tired of being taxed without representation in the British government.
- Through taxation many Americans felt that the British government threatened their livelihoods.
- Americans became so removed from the British homeland that they began to forge a new identity that was apart from the mother country.
- Acts of American rebellion like the Boston Tea Party and the Boston Massacre fueled the passions and anger of the colonists.
- American Founding Fathers like Franklin, Jefferson, and Adams popularized new ideas of government that were based on John Locke's philosophy. Traditional monarchies were rejected.
- American colonists became resentful of resources being shipped back to England.

Name _____

Date _____

Topic Generation with 6 Ideas – Linear Model

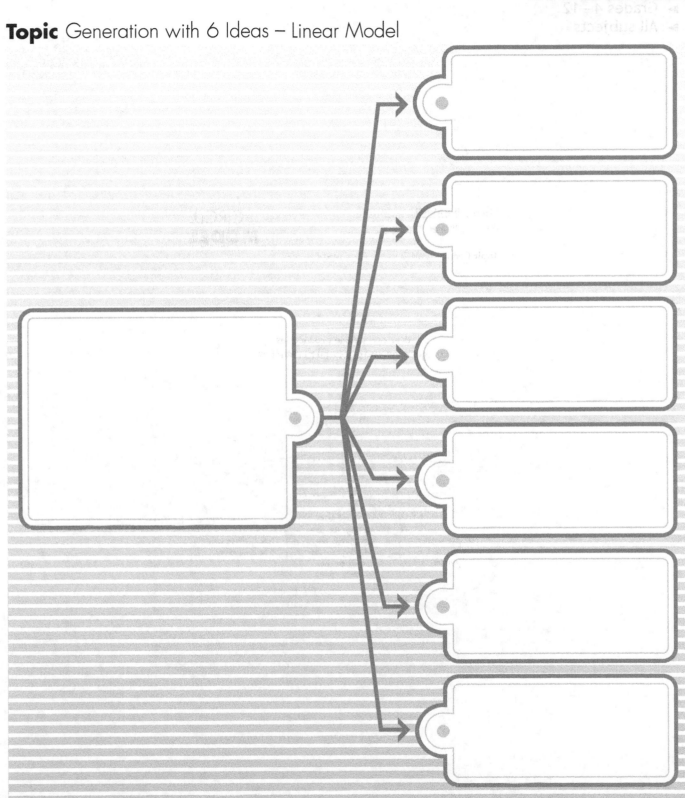

13 Topic Generation with 3 Ideas–Circle Model

▶ Grades 4–12
▶ All subjects

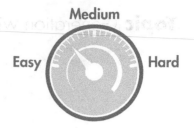

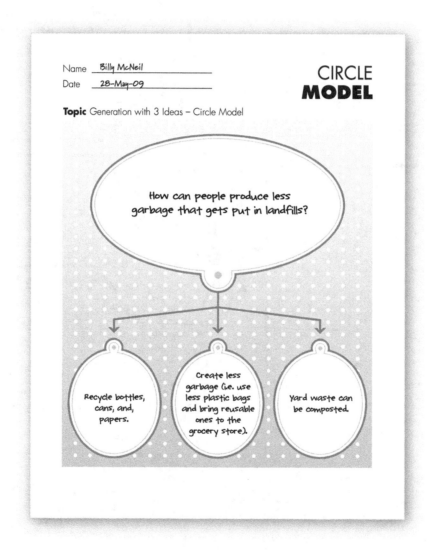

Name _____

Date _____

Topic Generation with 3 Ideas – Circle Model

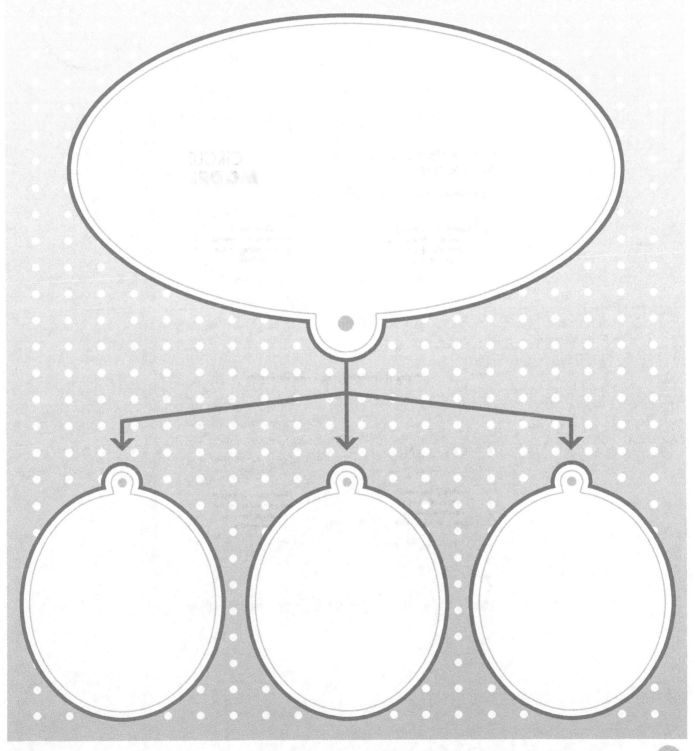

14 Topic Generation with 4 Ideas–Circle Model

▶ Grades 4–12
▶ All subjects

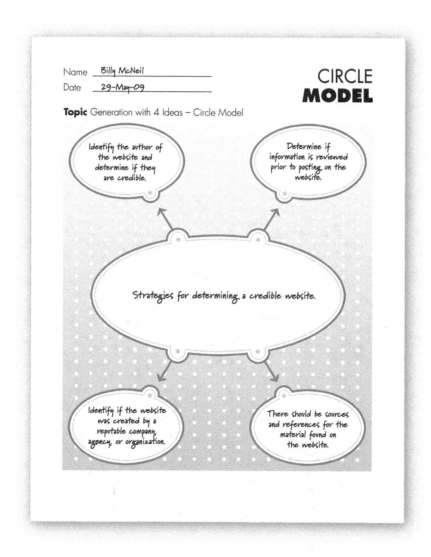

Name _____

Date _____

Topic Generation with 4 Ideas – Circle Model

15 Topic Generation with 6 Ideas—Circle Model

▶ Grades 4–12
▶ All subjects

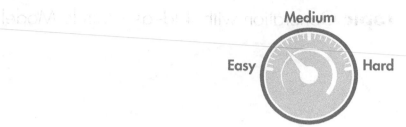

Easy • Medium • Hard

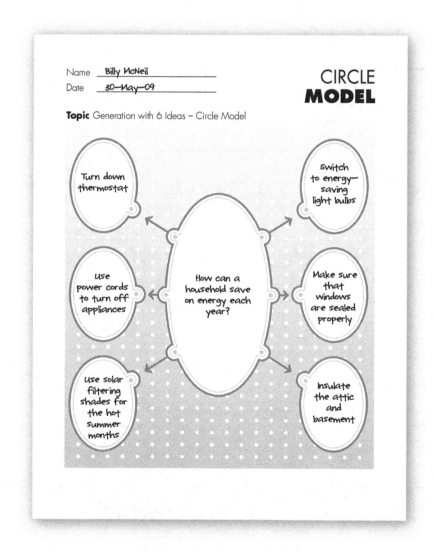

Name _____

Date _____

Topic Generation with 6 Ideas – Circle Model

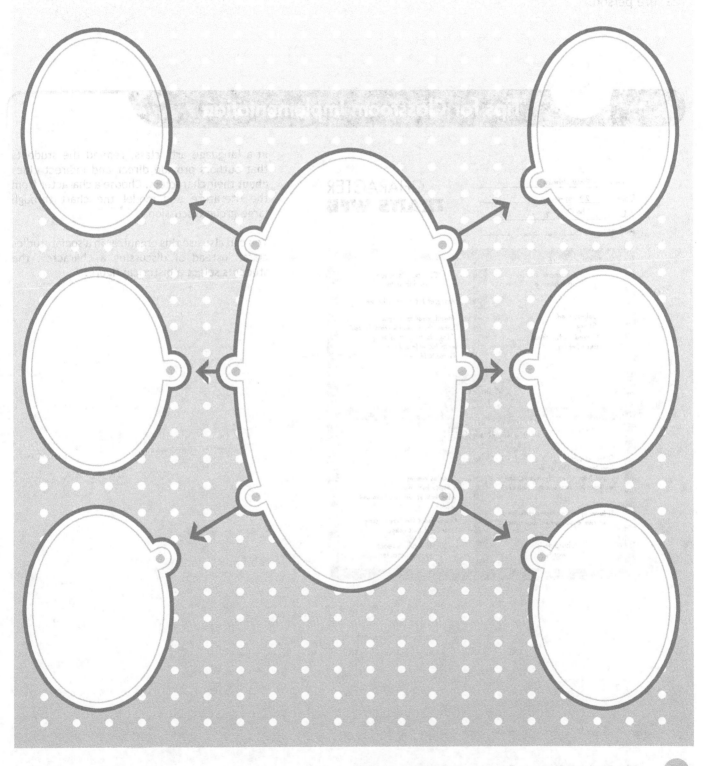

16 Character Traits Web

▶ Grades 4–12
▶ Social studies and English

The Character Traits Web organizer offers students another way to visually represent their ideas. The students collect attributes of a character or real-life person.

Medium
Easy   Hard

Tips for Classroom Implementation

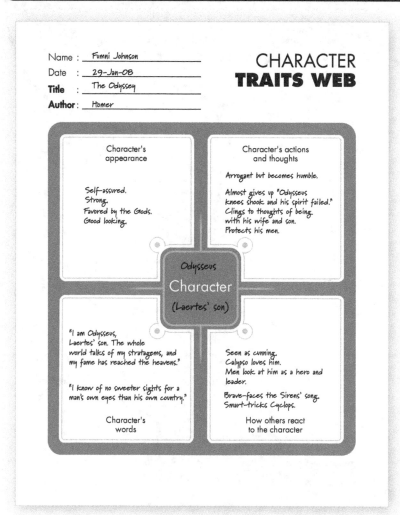

Name : Fumni Johnson
Date : 29-Jan-08
Title : The Odyssey
Author : Homer

CHARACTER
TRAITS WEB

Character's appearance

Self-assured.
Strong.
Favored by the Gods.
Good looking.

Character's actions and thoughts

Arrogant but becomes humble.

Almost gives up "Odysseus knees shook and his spirit failed."
Clings to thoughts of being with his wife and son.
Protects his men.

Odysseus
Character
(Laertes' son)

"I am Odysseus, Laertes' son. The whole world talks of my stratagems, and my fame has reached the heavens."

"I know of no sweeter sights for a man's own eyes than his own country."

Character's words

Seen as cunning.
Calypso loves him.
Men look at him as a hero and leader.

Brave-faces the Sirens' song.
Smart-tricks Cyclops.

How others react to the character

In a language arts class, remind the students that authors provide direct and indirect clues about their characters. Choose a character from the literature and model the chart through large-group discussion.

You can also use this organizer in a social studies class. Instead of discussing a character, the students select a historical figure.

Name : _____

Date : _____

Title : _____

Author : _____

CHARACTER
TRAITS WEB

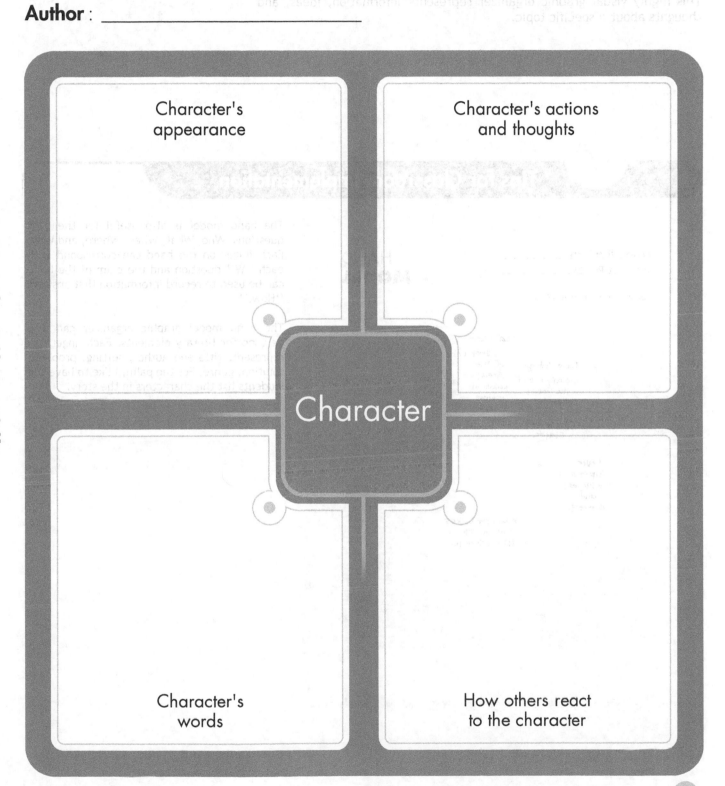

Character's
appearance

Character's actions
and thoughts

Character

Character's
words

How others react
to the character

17 Topic Generation: Hand Model

▶ Grades 4–6
▶ All subjects

This highly visual graphic organizer represents information, ideas, and thoughts about a specific topic.

Easy — Medium — Hard

 Tips for Classroom Implementation

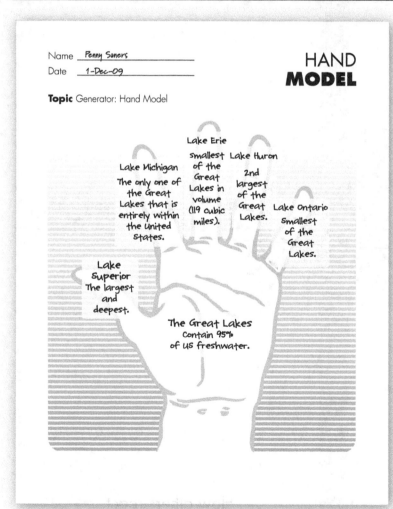

Name Penny Saners
Date 1-Dec-09

HAND MODEL

Topic Generator: Hand Model

Lake Erie
smallest of the Great Lakes in volume (119 cubic miles).

Lake Huron
2nd largest of the Great Lakes.

Lake Michigan
The only one of the Great Lakes that is entirely within the United States.

Lake Ontario
Smallest of the Great Lakes.

Lake Superior
The largest and deepest.

The Great Lakes Contain 95% of US freshwater.

The hand model is also useful for the 5 W questions: Who, What, When, Where, and Why. Each finger on the hand can correspond with each "W" question and the palm of the hand can be used to record information that answers "How."

The hand model graphic organizer can also be used for literary elements. Each finger can represent: title and author, setting, problem, solution, genre. For the palm, I like to have the students list the characters in the story.

Name _____

Date _____

Topic Generation: Hand Model

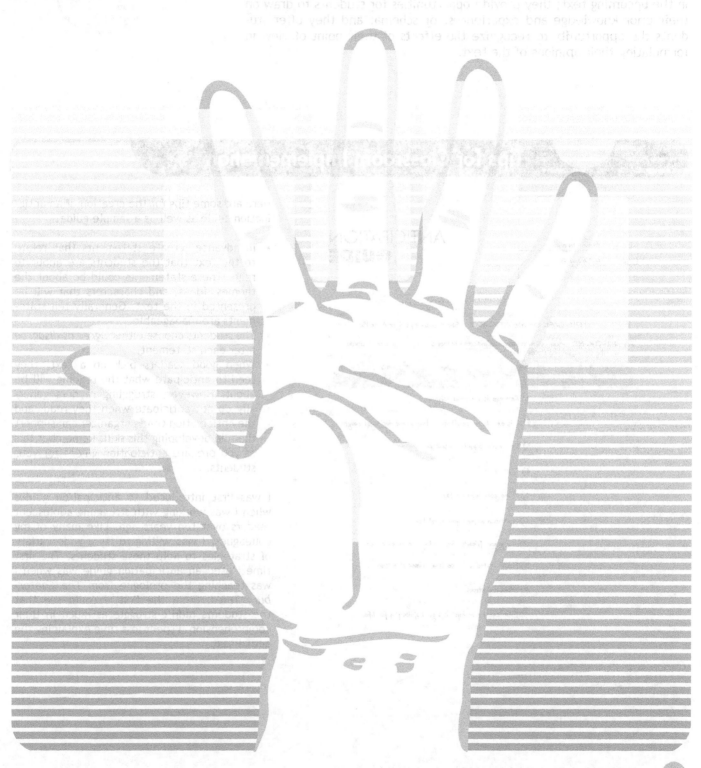

18 Anticipation Guide

▶ Grades 4–12
▶ All subjects

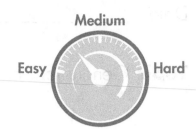

Medium
Easy   Hard

Anticipation guides are great prereading graphic organizers for the following reasons: they preview key themes and ideas that will be presented in the upcoming text; they provide opportunities for students to draw on their prior knowledge and experiences, or schema; and they offer students the opportunity to recognize the effects of their point of view in formulating their opinions of the text.

Tips for Classroom Implementation

Name _Annie Jarovich_

Date _9-Dec-08_

ANTICIPATION GUIDE

ANTICIPATION GUIDE

Topic | "THE CASK OF AMONTILLADO" A Short Story by Edgar Allen Poe

DIRECTIONS: Put an "X" in the space to indicate whether or not you agree or disagree with the corresponding statement.

Agree	Disagree	Statement
		1) Revenge is a learned behavior.
		2) It is o.k. to do something as long as you don't get caught.
		3) Time eases a guilty conscience.
		4) Trust no one.
		5) Pride goes before a fall.
		6) You should defend your reputation.
		7) Keep your friends close and your enemies closer.
		8) Premeditated is worse than crimes of passion.
		9) Greed destroys.
		10) An 'eye for an eye' is a good philosophy for life.

Here are some tips for the creation of an anticipation guide as well as a sample guide.

- In advance, create statements that relate to the text that the students are about to read. These statements could be about the themes, ideas, and characters that will be presented in the text. Generally ten statements are manageable.
- The students choose either *agree* or *disagree* after each statement.
- When good readers pick up a text, they tend to anticipate what the reading will be about. However, struggling readers generally do not anticipate when they read, and the Anticipation Guide organizer can support them in developing this skill. Remember this as you prepare anticipation guides for your students.

I was first introduced to anticipation guides when I was working with struggling adolescent readers over ten years ago. Like many of my colleagues, I was willing to try a wide variety of strategies to help these students. The first time I used an anticipation guide was when I was teaching the prologue from *The Canterbury Tales*. From the first, I could see that the students didn't struggle as much in their comprehension. I spent less time explaining the actual text.

Name _____

Date _____

ANTICIPATION
GUIDE

ANTICIPATION GUIDE

Topic _____

DIRECTIONS: Put an "X" in the space to indicate whether or not you agree or disagree with the corresponding statement.

Agree	Disagree	Statement

19 Hypothesis Guide

▶ Grades 4—12
▶ Social studies and science

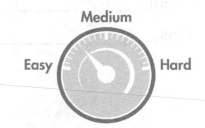

Especially useful for the science classroom, the Hypothesis Guide is a visualization structure for the scientific method. Guiding the students through the process of formulating a hypothesis reinforces the main concepts that are integral to the creation of a question or idea. Once the students create the question or idea, which is a hypothesis, they can test and evaluate it. As always, it is beneficial to model the graphic organizer for the students. This graphic organizer can be especially useful for lab experiments.

Tips for Classroom Implementation

Name   Portia Smith
Date   5-Dec-09

HYPOTHESIS GUIDE

Question
How does water impact plant growth?

Information
Food, sunlight and location can impact plant growth.
Use books, magazines and the internet to find information on plant growth.

Hypothesis
I predict that if a plant does not get enough water, it will die.

Test the hypothesis/data
Six plants: 2 with the recommended amount of water (control group) 2 plants with less than the required water and 2 with more than the required amount of water.

Results
The plants that received less water did not grow as well as the ones that received the correct and recommended amount of water.

Conclusions
Plants need different amounts of water to grow well and the plants that received the recommended water grew the best.

A scientific experiment may comprise the following:

1. When you observe something, you may have questions about that phenomenon. State your QUESTION.
2. Gather as much INFORMATION as you can about your question.
3. Find out what information has already been discovered about your question.
4. Formulate a HYPOTHESIS. Write a statement that predicts what may happen in your experiment.
5. Test your hypothesis. Design an experiment to test your hypothesis.
6. Perform the experiment.
7. Collect DATA. Record the results of the investigation.
8. Summarize RESULTS. Analyze the data and note trends in your experimental results.
9. Draw CONCLUSIONS. Determine whether or not the data support the hypothesis of your experiment.

Name _____

Date _____

HYPOTHESIS
GUIDE

Question

Information

Hypothesis

Test the hypothesis/data

Results

Conclusions

20 Idea Web

▶ Grades 4—12
▶ All subjects

An idea web allows learners to organize information in a visual format. Unlike a standard linear outline, the idea web makes the connections among ideas and details more evident.

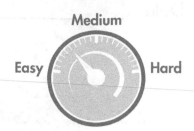

Medium

Easy   Hard

Tips for Classroom Implementation

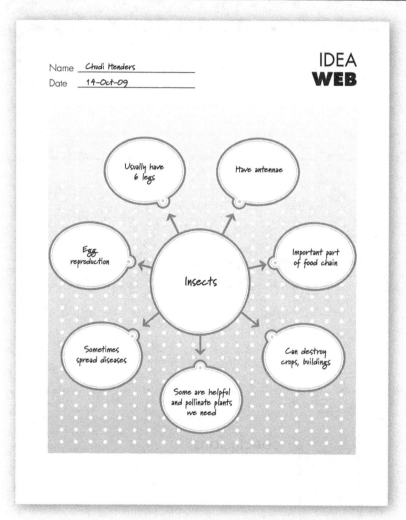

A highly adaptable organizer, the Idea Web can be used as an opening brainstorming activity through large group discussion. You can use large chart paper or an overhead projector to record the students' ideas. Students can also use an idea web for prewriting or to tap into prior knowledge at the beginning of an instructional unit.

Name _____

Date _____

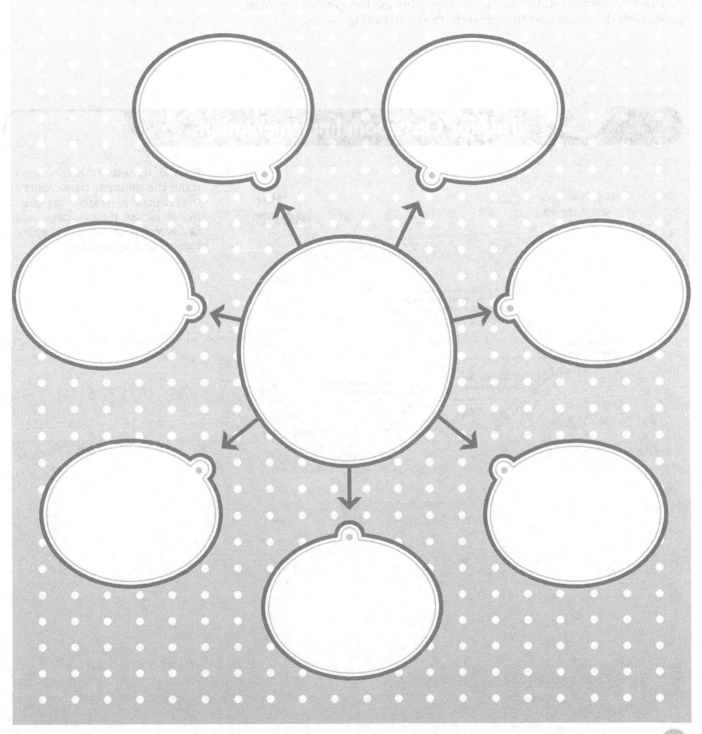

21 Fishbone

▶ Grades 4–12
▶ All subjects

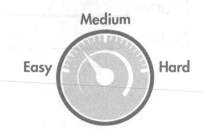

The Fishbone (also known as the Cause and Effect Diagram or Ishikawa Diagram) is named after its Japanese inventor, Kaoru Ishikawa (1915–1989). Use the Fishbone to determine the causal relationships in a complex idea or event. This organizer helps students understand how a central theme can have numerous related ideas. To effectively use this graphic organizer, begin with the result and then analyze the contributing causes.

Tips for Classroom Implementation

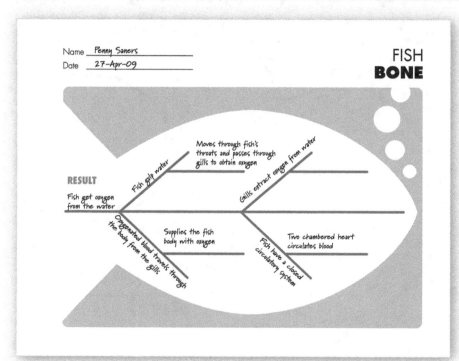

For the students to better understand the different components of this structured graphic organizer, model its use through large-group discussion prior to the students' independent application.

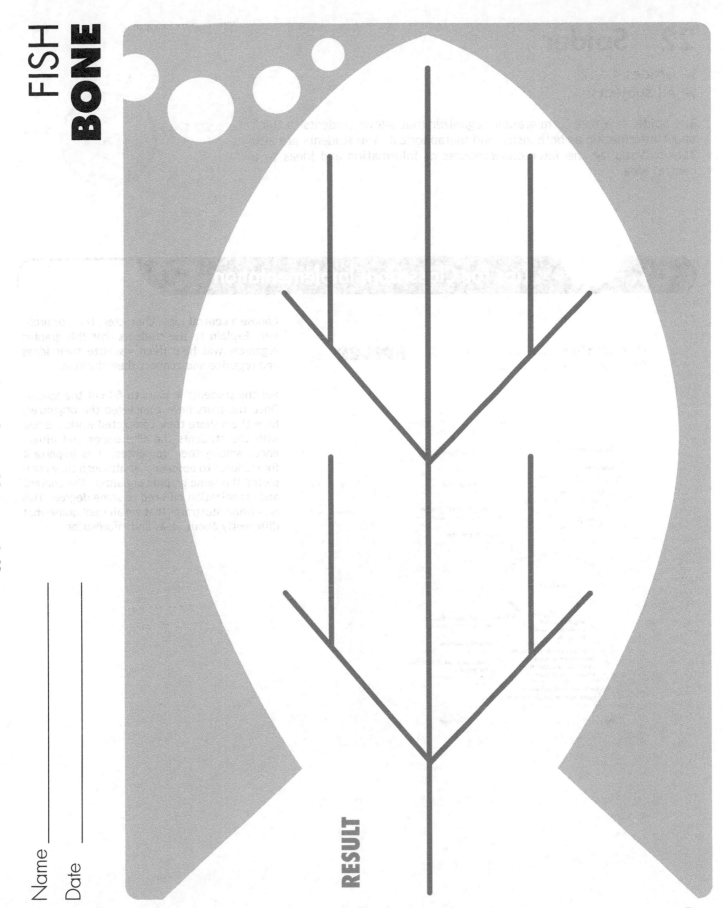

FISH
BONE

Name _____

Date _____

RESULT

22 Spider

▶ Grades 4–12
▶ All subjects

The Spider is a free-form graphic organizer that allows students to think about information as both visual and metaphorical. The students are also able to visualize the interconnectedness of information and ideas to a central idea.

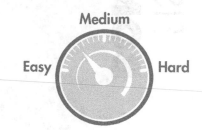

Medium
Easy   Hard

Tips for Classroom Implementation

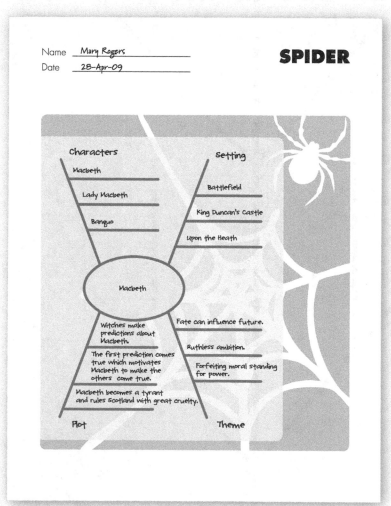

Name Mary Rogers
Date 28-Apr-09

SPIDER

Characters
Macbeth
Lady Macbeth
Banquo

Setting
Battlefield
King Duncan's Castle
Upon the Heath

Macbeth

Witches make predictions about Macbeth.

The first prediction comes true which motivates Macbeth to make the others come true.

Macbeth becomes a tyrant and rules Scotland with great cruelty.

Fate can influence future.

Ruthless ambition.

Forfeiting moral standing for power.

Plot

Theme

Choose a central idea, character, text, or problem. Explain to the students that this graphic organizer will help them visualize their ideas and organize and connect their thinking.

Put the students in pairs to fill out the Spider. Once the pairs have completed the organizer, have them share their completed work. Discuss with the students the similarities and differences among their responses. It is important for students to observe that although they completed the same graphic organizer, the content and organization differed to some degree. This is fine and illustrates that we all think somewhat differently about ideas and information.

Name _____

Date _____

SPIDER

23 Herringbone

▶ Grades 4–12
▶ All subjects

The Herringbone graphic organizer is used for establishing supporting details for a main idea. It can be used to organize information for all content areas.

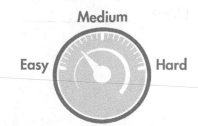

Easy   Medium   Hard

Tips for Classroom Implementation

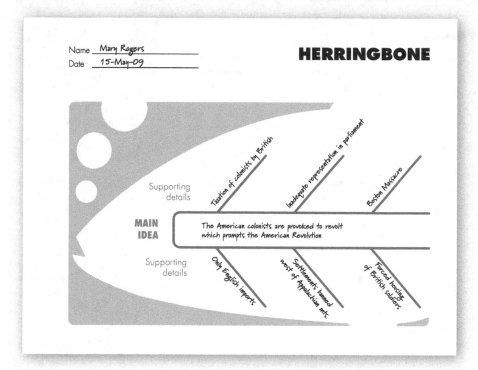

Name _Mary Rogers_
Date _15-May-09_

HERRINGBONE

Supporting details
- Taxation of colonists by British
- Inadequate representation in parliament
- Boston Massacre

MAIN IDEA
The American colonists are provoked to revolt which prompts the American Revolution

Supporting details
- Only English imports
- Settlements banned west of Appalachian mts.
- Forced housing of British soldiers

Students will benefit from your modeling the use of this graphic organizer on an overhead projector or chart paper.

Learning how to organize and classify information is an important skill for all students. Students are asked to organize and classify information every day. When students read, they should be encouraged to read and classify information. Students can use this graphic organizer when taking notes for assigned reading as a way to organize and classify new information.

HERRINGBONE

Name _____

Date _____

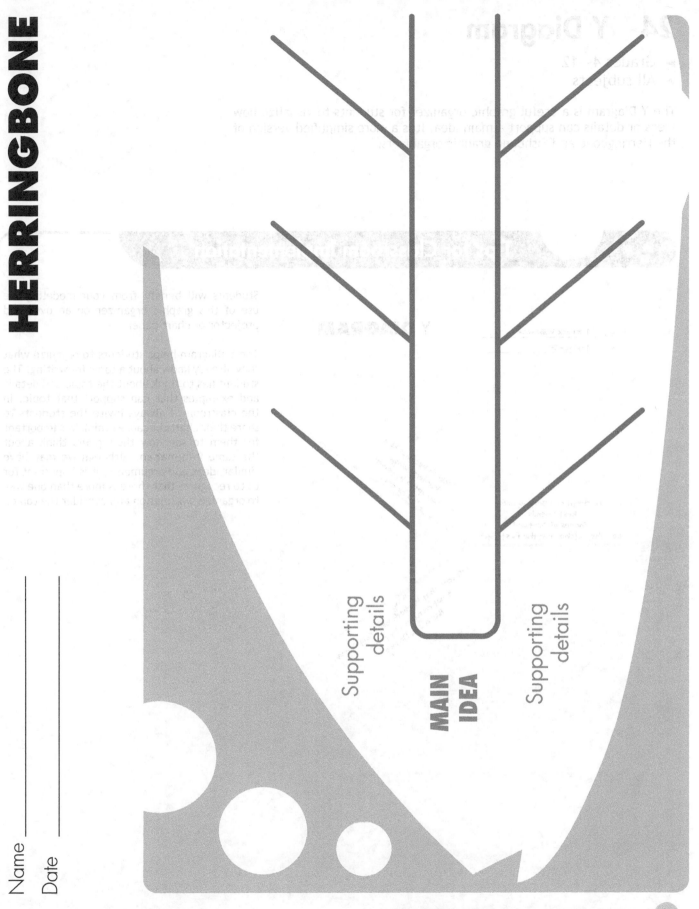

Supporting details

MAIN IDEA

Supporting details

24   Y Diagram

▶ Grades 4—12
▶ All subjects

The Y Diagram is a useful graphic organizer for students to visualize how ideas or details can support a main idea. It is a more simplified version of the Herringbone and Fishbone graphic organizers.

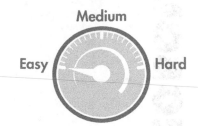

Tips for Classroom Implementation

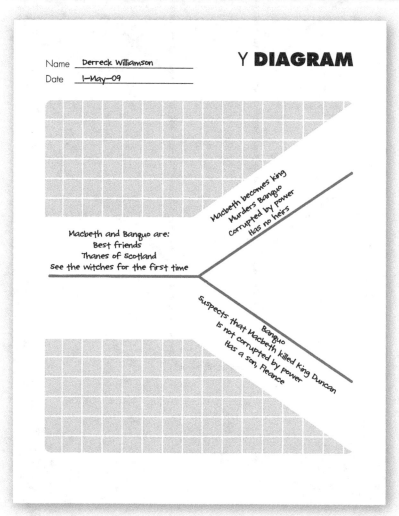

Students will benefit from your modeling the use of this graphic organizer on an overhead projector or chart paper.

The Y Diagram helps students to organize what they already know about a topic for writing. The student has to think about the topic and details and examples that can support that topic. In the classroom, I always invite the students to share their charts because I think it is important for them to see how their peers think about the same information. Although we may have similar ideas and arguments, it is important for us to recognize that there is more than one way to organize information and consider the topic.

Y **DIAGRAM**

Name _____

Date _____

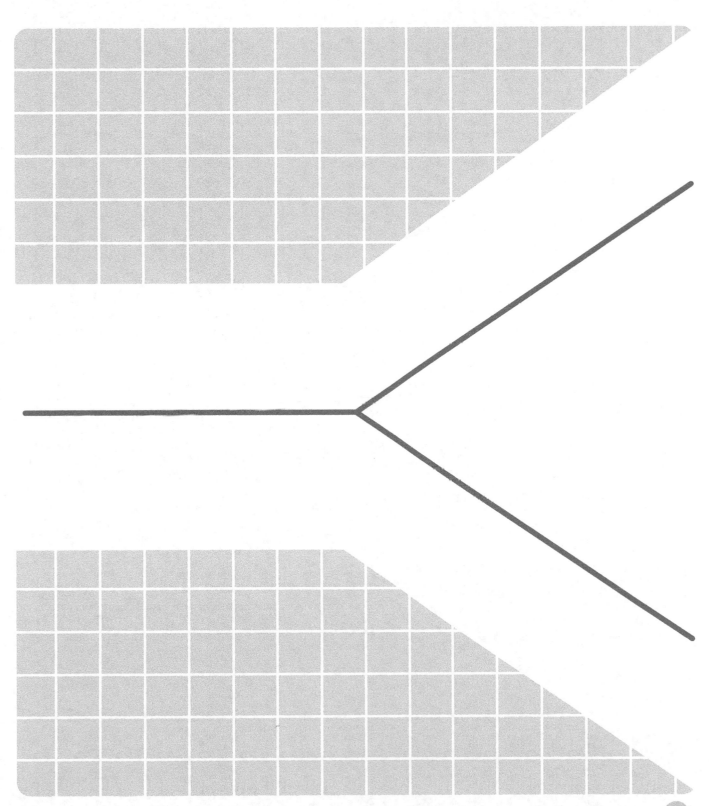

Y DIAGRAM

CHAPTER THREE

Graphic Organizers for Vocabulary Development

A special note on this chapter: As mentioned in Chapter One, all of these graphic organizers can be used as templates for a vocabulary log or notebook. These organizers become a student-created vocabulary reference book to which the students can refer during the course of the school year.

25 Vocabulary Slide

▶ Grades 5–12
▶ Social studies, English, science, health, mathematics

It is quite likely that most of us were taught vocabulary by being given long lists of words; we were required to write down the definition for each word and write a sentence using the vocabulary word. Once we had memorized these words, they were given on a quiz, usually on a Friday. Today we know that this is not the most effective way to teach vocabulary. Instead, vocabulary lessons must be *contextual*.

Simply put: the more students manipulate and use a new word, the more likely it will become part of their vocabulary. Vocabulary slides prompt students to use and apply newly encountered words. When students study fewer words in greater depth, as they do with the vocabulary slide, they are learning how language works. The sections of the slide require the students to examine the etymology and the part of speech, to find a synonym and antonym, and to use the word in an original sentence. These applications enable students to connect to and process the word through several tasks.

Tips for Classroom Implementation

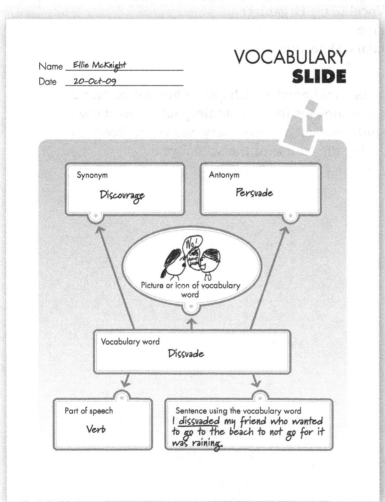

You can have students create vocabulary slides from self-identified words in the assigned reading, or you can assign words. You can also use the vocabulary slides as flash cards that the students use for review.

The first time that I required eleventh-grade students in a British literature class to create vocabulary slides, the students were a bit surprised when I asked them to draw pictures of the vocabulary words. What I noticed was that the students had to internally process the vocabulary in order to create visual representations of the words' meanings. As a result, I witnessed greater transference in the students' writing and improved ability to recognize the newly acquired vocabulary words.

Name _____

Date _____

VOCABULARY
SLIDE

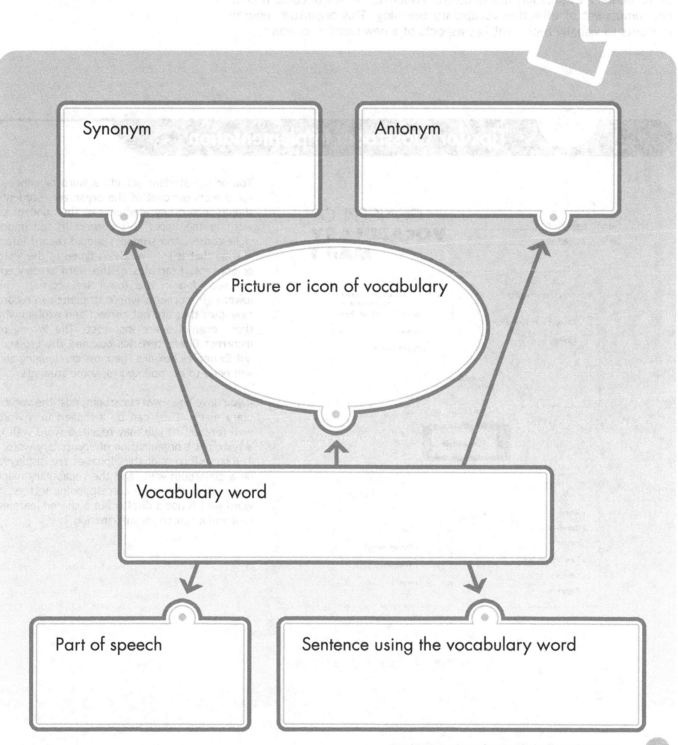

Synonym

Antonym

Picture or icon of vocabulary

Vocabulary word

Part of speech

Sentence using the vocabulary word

26 Concept or Vocabulary Map I

▶ Grades 5–12
▶ Social studies, English, science, health, mathematics

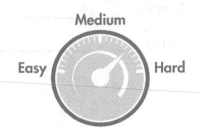

Students often memorize definitions rather than study words or concepts in depth. When students study words from different perspectives, they are more likely to internalize the new vocabulary. Our understanding of vocabulary acquisition has evolved. Visualization has become a critical component of effective vocabulary teaching. This organizer requires students to visually represent key aspects of a new word or concept.

Tips for Classroom Implementation

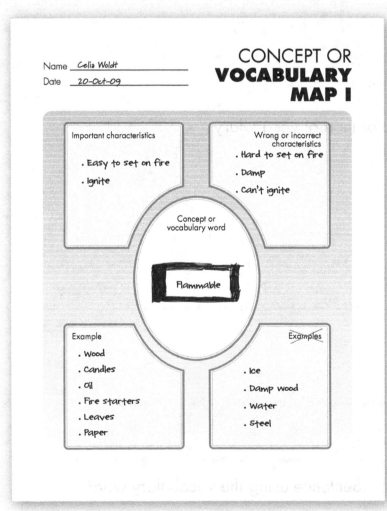

You or the student selects a word or concept for the center oval of the organizer. Students should record key elements of the concept or word in the upper left corner. In the upper right corner, the students should record information that is incorrectly assigned to the word or concept. Examples of the word or concept are recorded in the lower left corner. The lower right corner is where students can record examples that are not correct and explain why these examples are incorrect. The Wrong or Incorrect Characteristics box and the crossed-out Examples box are the most challenging and will need to be modeled for some students.

If you have your own classroom, post the vocabulary maps. They can be arranged in a word wall format. As you may recall, a word wall is a systematic organization of vocabulary words. The large letters of the alphabet are displayed on a classroom wall, and the vocabulary maps are posted under the corresponding letters. A word wall is not a display but a shared learning tool and a source for information.

Name _____

Date _____

CONCEPT OR
VOCABULARY
MAP I

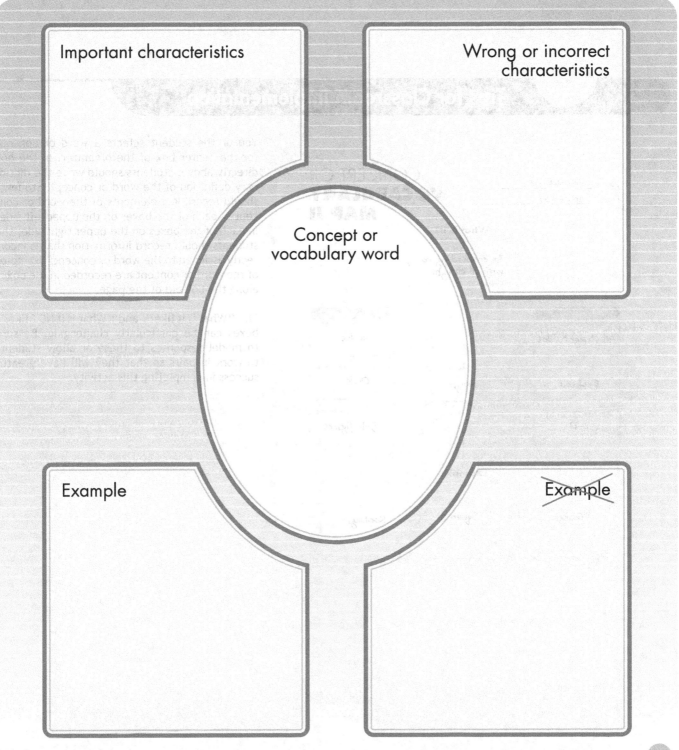

Important characteristics

Wrong or incorrect characteristics

Concept or vocabulary word

Example

Example

27 Concept or Vocabulary Map II

▶ Grades 5–12
▶ Social studies, English, science, health, mathematics

This version is different from Concept or Vocabulary Map I in that it is more explicit about the placement of information and requires an exact definition for the vocabulary word or concept.

 Tips for Classroom Implementation

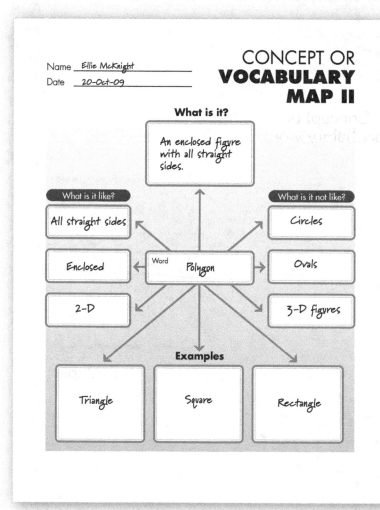

Name _Ellie McKnight_
Date _20-Oct-09_

CONCEPT OR VOCABULARY MAP II

What is it?

An enclosed figure with all straight sides.

What is it like?

All straight sides

Enclosed

2-D

Word Polygon

What is it not like?

Circles

Ovals

3-D figures

Examples

Triangle

Square

Rectangle

You or the student selects a word or concept for the center box of the organizer. In the box directly above, students should write the dictionary definition of the word or concept. Students should record key elements of the word or concept in each of the boxes on the upper left side. In each of the boxes on the upper right side, the students should record information that is incorrectly assigned to the word or concept. Examples of the word or concept are recorded in the boxes along the bottom of the page.

The "What is it like?" and "What is it NOT like?" boxes can be particularly challenging. Be sure to model responses to these or allow students to work in pairs so that they will have greater success in completing this activity.

CONCEPT OR VOCABULARY MAP II

Name _____

Date _____

What is it?

[box]

What is it like?

[box]

[box]

[box]

Word

What is it not like?

[box]

[box]

[box]

Examples

[box]

[box]

[box]

28 Concept or Vocabulary Map III

▶ Grades 5–12
▶ Social studies, English, science, health, mathematics

This version of the concept or vocabulary map requires students to include an illustration or visualization.

Medium

Easy — Hard

Tips for Classroom Implementation

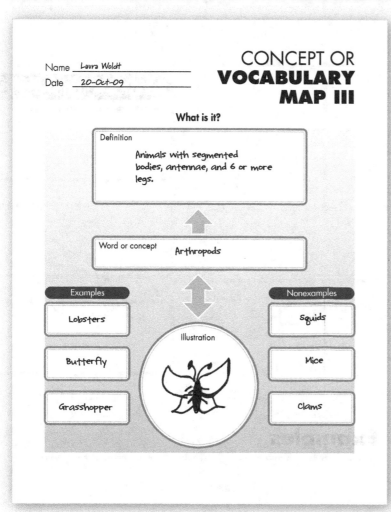

Name Laura Woldt
Date 20-Oct-09

CONCEPT OR
**VOCABULARY
MAP III**

What is it?

Definition
Animals with segmented bodies, antennae, and 6 or more legs.

Word or concept Arthropods

Examples

Lobsters

Butterfly

Grasshopper

Illustration

Nonexamples

Squids

Mice

Clams

You or the student selects a word or concept for the center box of the organizer. Above the word or concept box, students should write the definition in the provided space. They should record key elements of the concept or word in each of the boxes on the left side. In each of the boxes on the right side, the students should record information that is incorrectly assigned to the word or concept. They should place a picture or icon that visualizes the word or concept in the oval at the bottom.

This organizer is particularly helpful with concrete nouns similar to those that you would find in a science textbook.

CONCEPT OR
VOCABULARY
MAP III

Name _____

Date _____

What is it?

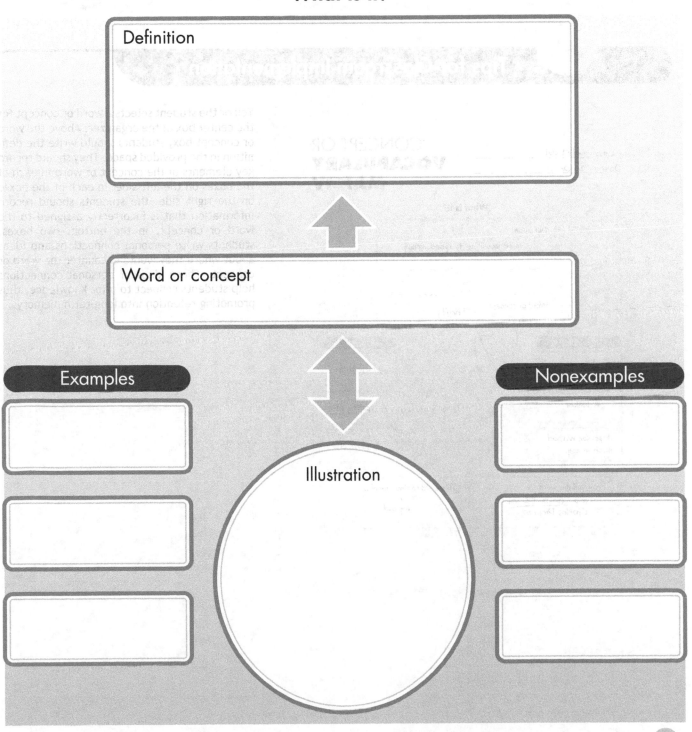

Definition

Word or concept

Examples

Nonexamples

Illustration

29 Concept or Vocabulary Map IV

► Grades 5–12
► Social studies, English, science, health, mathematics

This version of the concept or vocabulary map requires a personal connection with the new vocabulary word or concept.

Medium
Easy   Hard

Tips for Classroom Implementation

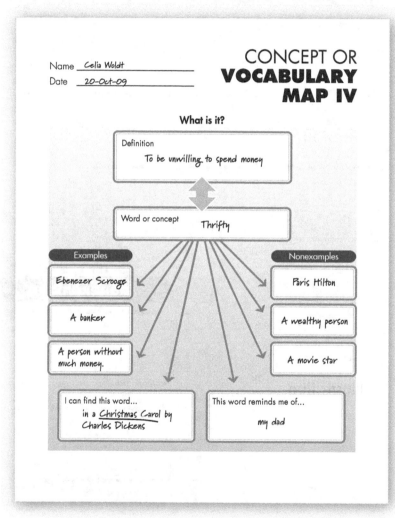

You or the student selects a word or concept for the center box of the organizer. Above the word or concept box, students should write the definition in the provided space. They should record key elements of the concept or word in each of the boxes on the left side. In each of the boxes on the right side, the students should record information that is incorrectly assigned to the word or concept. In the bottom two boxes, students write personal connections and ideas about where they would encounter the word or concept. These kinds of personal connections help students connect to prior knowledge, thus promoting retention into long-term memory.

Name _____

Date _____

CONCEPT OR VOCABULARY MAP IV

What is it?

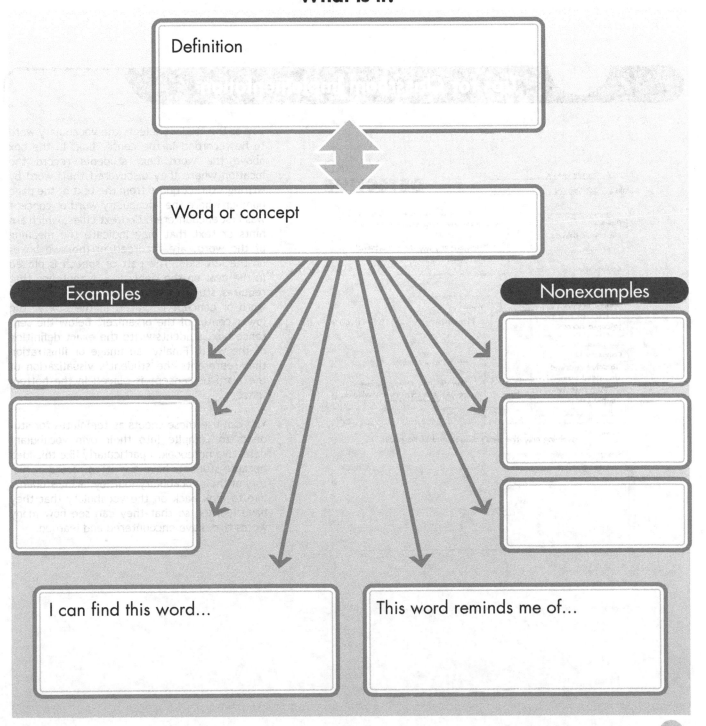

Definition

Word or concept

Examples

Nonexamples

I can find this word...

This word reminds me of...

30 Word Detective

► Grades 5—12
► Social studies, English, science, health, mathematics

The importance of encouraging students to study words cannot be emphasized enough. In this graphic organizer, students are prompted to research the etymology of words and connect visual images to the words that they encounter.

Tips for Classroom Implementation

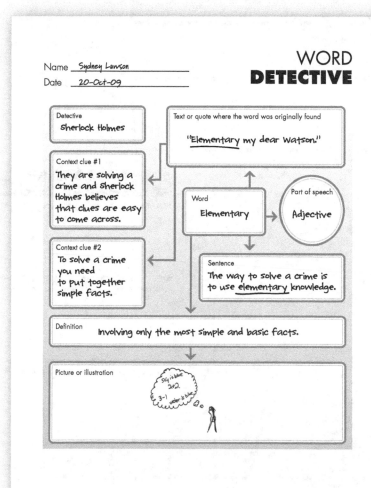

You or the student selects the vocabulary word to be recorded in the center box. In the box above the word box, students record the location where they discovered their word by writing a direct quote from the text or the page number where the vocabulary word or concept was first encountered. Context clues, which are hints or text that may indicate the meaning of the word, are recorded in the two boxes on the left side. The part of speech is placed in the oval on the right side. A sentence that requires students to use the new vocabulary word or concept is placed in the box at the lower center of the organizer. Below the sentence box, students write the exact definition of the word. Finally, an image or illustration that represents the student's visualization of the word or concept is placed in the bottom space.

You can use these sheets as templates for students to compile into their own vocabulary detective notebook. I particularly like this idea because students have a written record or history of their vocabulary journey. Many students like to look back on the vocabulary that they have learned so that they can see how many words they have encountered and learned.

WORD DETECTIVE

Name _____

Date _____

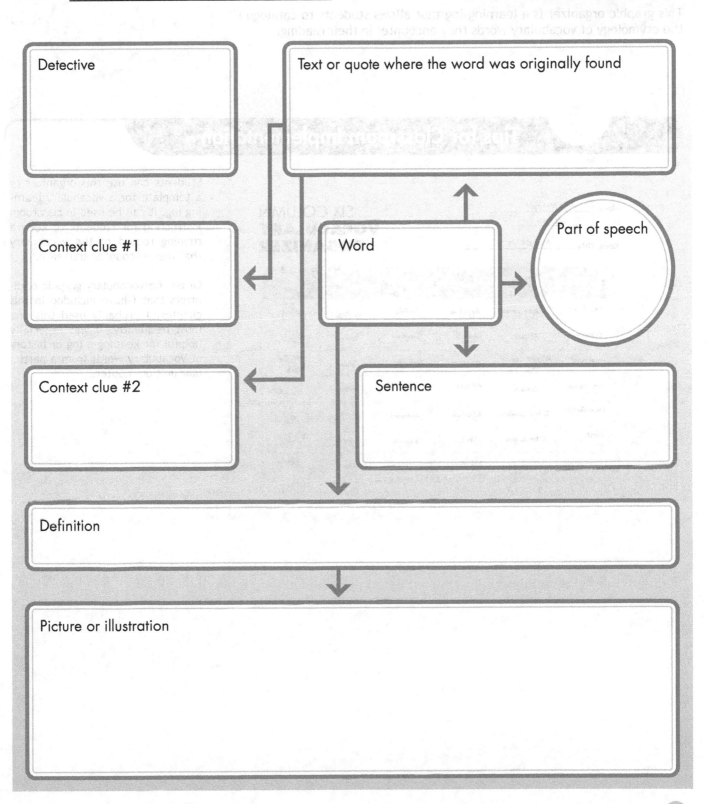

Detective

Text or quote where the word was originally found

Context clue #1

Word

Part of speech

Context clue #2

Sentence

Definition

Picture or illustration

31 Six-Column Vocabulary Organizer

▶ Grades 5–12
▶ Social studies, English, science, health, mathematics

This graphic organizer is a learning log that allows students to catalogue the etymology of vocabulary words they encounter in their reading.

Medium

Easy   Hard

Tips for Classroom Implementation

Name ___Ellie McKnight___

Date ___6/16/09___

Book Title ___Midnight Sun___

SIX COLUMN VOCABULARY ORGANIZER

Vocabulary word	Sentence dictionary definition	Part of speech	Synonym	Antonym	Picture or icon that represents the word
Monotonous	Lacking variety	Adjective	Tedious	Exciting	
Occasionally	At times	Adverb	Sometimes	Never	2+5
Incoherent	Without logic or meaning	Adjective	Disjointed	Rational	
Unconscious	Unaware	Adjective	Asleep	Awake	z z z
Uncomfortable	To lack comfort	Adjective	Awkward	Calm	This chair is not comfortable
Burst	To break open	Verb	To explode	Assemble	Boom
Excruciating	Very painful	Adjective	Unbearable	Calm	ouch!

Students can use this organizer as a template for a vocabulary learning log. It can be used in classroom instruction for students to keep a running record of the vocabulary that they encounter and learn.

Of all the vocabulary graphic organizers that I have included in this chapter, I probably used this one most frequently. It was especially helpful for keeping a log or history of vocabulary words from a particular unit or chapter.

Name _____

Date _____

Book Title _____

SIX COLUMN
VOCABULARY
ORGANIZER

Vocabulary word	Sentence dictionary definition	Part of speech	Synonym	Antonym	Picture or icon that represents the word

32 Vocabulary Tree

▶ Grades 5—12
▶ Social studies, English, science, health, mathematics

This highly visual graphic organizer requires students to specify a root word and related words, a strategy that supports students in learning and understanding new vocabulary.

Easy   Medium   Hard

Tips for Classroom Implementation

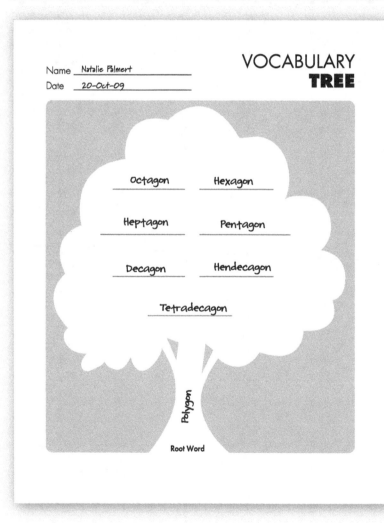

Name Natalie Palmert

Date 20-Oct-09

VOCABULARY TREE

Octagon   Hexagon

Heptagon   Pentagon

Decagon   Hendecagon

Tetradecagon

Polygon

Root Word

In addition to using this graphic organizer as a means to show how words can relate to a root word, I have also used this graphic organizer for expository writing. The students can use the main trunk for their thesis and the upper spaces to list details and evidence to prove the thesis.

I have also used the tree graphic organizer as a prereading activity. The students will write their main prediction about the text they are about to read on the trunk and then use the upper spaces for details and examples from the text to prove or disprove their prediction.

Name _____

Date _____

Root Word

33 Cyber Vocabulary Detective

► Grades 5–12
► Social studies, English, science, health, mathematics

Oftentimes vocabulary words are assigned to students at the beginning of an instructional unit. This organizer prompts the students to find the assigned words on the Internet and to use this information to determine the meanings of the assigned vocabulary.

Tips for Classroom Implementation

Name _____Eleanor Rigby_____

Date _____June 29, 2009_____

CYBER VOCABULARY DETECTIVE

DIRECTIONS: As you look for your vocabulary words in the assigned Web sites, it is helpful to use the FIND command. For each of the assigned vocabulary words, write the sentence from the Web site where you find the word. Guess what the word might mean.

Web Site Name: _____Yahoo, Finance_____

Vocabulary word	Sentence that includes vocabulary word	What might the vocabulary word mean?
Confectionery	The global confectionery market accounted for 50 billion in retail sales last year.	All types of candy
Capita	Americans consume 25 lbs of candy per capita annually.	A prominent part
Abstemious	Abstemious, positively with the average consumption of 16 lbs.....	Moderate
Discretionary	The global economic downturn may have caused many consumers to cut discretionary spending.	You can do what you want with it
Penetrate	Some beetles can penetrate wood.	To pierce through
Recession	Recessions happen when the stock market crashes.	When there is no growth in the economy
Skirmishes	In our school there are very few skirmishes.	Fights

Give the students a list of Internet sites that will assist them in researching the vocabulary. The students can work in pairs to complete the organizer.

Here are some sites that I recommend for vocabulary research.

Dictionary.com. This site offers a standard English language dictionary.

etymonline.com. This site describes the origins of words rather than supplying a traditional or straight definition.

Word.com. Sponsored by Merriam-Webster, this site offers complete information about words.

I am a big fan of this strategy for many reasons. Effectively using technology in classrooms helps all kinds of learners. Exploring Web sites to learn and study vocabulary is engaging because it is highly visual and resembles what people do in the "real world" to gather information; further, many Web sites provide audio support, which is particularly helpful for English language learners and students who have speech or language needs. The audio-supported Web sites often provide pronunciations of the words and have auditory files for definitions and sample sentences.

Name _____

Date _____

CYBER
VOCABULARY
DETECTIVE

DIRECTIONS: As you look for your vocabulary words in the assigned Web sites, it is helpful to use the FIND command. For each of the assigned vocabulary words, write the sentence from the Web site where you find the word. Guess what the word might mean.

Web Site Name: _____

Vocabulary word	Sentence that includes vocabulary word	What might the vocabulary word mean?

CHAPTER FOUR

Graphic Organizers for Note Taking
and Study Skills

34 Cornell Notes

▶ Grades 5–12

▶ Social studies, English, science, health, mathematics

Developed by Walter Pauk, an education professor at Cornell University in the 1950s, Cornell Notes is a widely used and accepted strategy for taking notes. The students should take notes in the right-hand column of the organizer; the left-hand column is for corresponding questions, main points, or ideas. The bottom space prompts students to summarize the information they have recorded.

Tips for Classroom Implementation

Name Penny Lane

Date June 29, 2009

CORNELL NOTES

Topic Legally Blonde, The Musical

Questions/key points	Notes
Why is the title Legally Blonde? Why did she go to law school? Why is there a Greek chorus?	• Because a blonde went to law school and she wants a right to be blonde. • Because she wanted to win back her ex-boyfriend. • Because they wanted to add some of the vintage Broadway elements.

Summary

This article is about the musical Legally Blonde. It reviews how the characters make the musical much more entertaining and how it is fun.

Model this strategy for the students and remind them of the five Rs of note taking:

1. *Record* the most important or emphasized information.
2. *Reduce* and synthesize information wherever possible, making it as concise as you can.
3. *Recite:* read your notes aloud.
4. *Reflect* and consider how this information is connected to your personal experiences and what you already know.
5. *Review:* look over your notes more than once.

Cornell Notes are most frequently used at the high school level. Oftentimes when we assign textbooks for our students to read, they are faced with text that is densely packed with information. Cornell Notes are a structure that helps students pull out the key ideas and details.

Name _____

Date _____

CORNELL
NOTES

Topic _____

Questions/key points

Notes

Summary

35 Three-Column Notes

▶ Grades 5–12
▶ Social studies, English, science, health, mathematics

This strategy should be used as a *during reading* or *after reading* activity. For a *during reading* activity, you and students complete the organizer together. The first column is used to record the topic of the text or discussion. In the second column, students should record what they learned from reading the text or from discussion. In the third column, the students will write their ideas and opinions as they reflect on the information about the topic. Make sure that you model the strategy and explain how to use the column note structure.

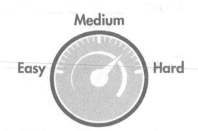

Medium

Easy   Hard

Tips for Classroom Implementation

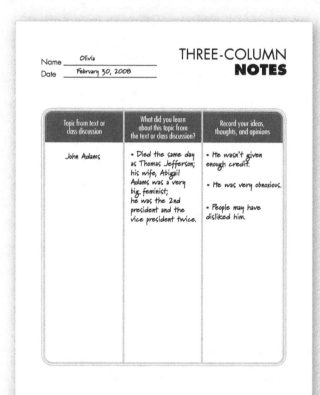

As the students progress from the first column to the 3rd, explain that they are carefully narrowing the topic. The first column will have the main topic recorded and as they progress to the second and third document, there will be more details and text. The third column should be visually "packed" with details and information. For some students, offering a visual like sand passing through a funnel, this can aid their understanding.

THREE-COLUMN NOTES

Name _____

Date _____

Topic from text or class discussion	What did you learn about this topic from the text or class discussion?	Record your ideas, thoughts, and opinions

36   T Notes

▶ Grades 5–12
▶ Social studies, English, science, health, mathematics

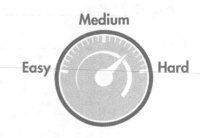

This graphic organizer facilitates students' ability to compare ideas and concepts. Use the space at the bottom of the organizer page for students to record their opinions about the ideas and to summarize the recorded information. The students identify key ideas and concepts, and as they record this information, they begin to develop language for the comparison of ideas. Students also learn how to extend ideas and information as they record parallels on each side of the graphic organizer. For example, when a statement or fact is recorded in the left-hand column, a parallel is required in the right-hand column. The students' experience in creating notes with the T Notes graphic organizer prepares them to write compare-contrast compositions.

Tips for Classroom Implementation

You should model this graphic organizer for the students. Using different colored markers or pens for each area of the graphic organizer is an effective way to emphasize the different kinds of information.

T NOTES

Name _____ Joe Brown _____
Date _____ 12/1/08 _____

Global Warming

Problems	Solutions
– Kills animals	– Conserve habitats
– Melting ice	– Diminish greenhouse gases
– Messes up environment	– Plants, trees, etc.
– Rising sea-level	– Conserve energy
– Hole in ozone layer	– Don't fish a lot

Name _____

Date _____

37 Analysis Notes

► Grades 5–12
► English

One of the greatest obstacles for struggling readers is the ability to pull out main ideas and details from a narrative text. Plot analysis notes prompt the reader to identify important information while applying elements of plot. Plot analysis notes are quite different from a multiple-choice assessment in that students need to know and *apply* literary elements to a narrative text.

Tips for Classroom Implementation

Name _____

Date _____

ANALYSIS NOTES

Categories: → Traits/Characteristics ↓	Macbeth	Lady Macbeth	Banquo	King Duncan	Malcolm
Ambitious and wants power	●	●			
Related to Macbeth		●			
Macbeth's friend			●		
Sees the Three Weird Sisters	●		●		
Member of Scottish Royalty				●	●
Related to King Duncan					●

You will need to model this graphic organizer. Instruct the students that they must determine what is important from the text. Let the students know that there may be instances when all the plot elements cannot be applied. This is an effective tool for assessing students' reading comprehension. In general terms, the more the students are able to add detail and personal comments to their notes, the greater their comprehension of the text.

Review with the students the elements of plot:

Exposition: Usually reveals the time, setting, and c introduce the characters.

Rising Action: An inciting event and foreshadowing are often in the rising action and ends with the climax.

Climax: The turning point of the story.

Falling Action: The events after the climax that leads to the end of the story (resolution).

Resolution: Concludes the action of the story.

ANALYSIS **NOTES**

Name

Date

Categories:

Traits/Characteristics

38 Summary Organizer

▶ Grades 5—12
▶ Social studies, English, science, health

This graphic organizer prompts students to create main categories, supply relevant details, and write a summary. The organizer develops the students' skills in identifying key information and providing details that facilitate comprehension.

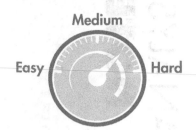

Tips for Classroom Implementation

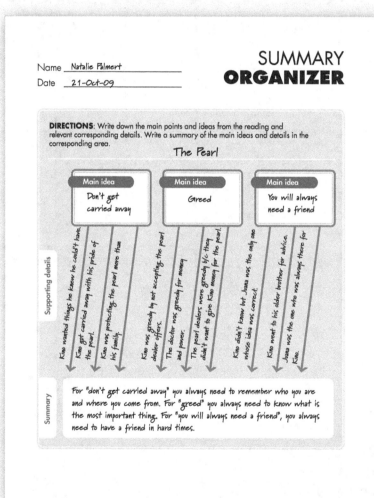

You will need to model this graphic organizer for students and explain how it prepares them for assignments like quizzes and tests.

Summarizing plays an important role in learning. On one level, by asking students to summarize important ideas, information, or text, you are checking to make sure that they understand content. Yet on another level, by summarizing what they have learned, students are also opening the door to reflection. When students reflect on what they have learned, they begin to understand why the newly acquired information is so meaningful. This organizer maps out the details that lead students to reflect and to create a summarizing statement.

Name _____

Date _____

DIRECTIONS: Write down the main points and ideas from the reading and relevant corresponding details. Write a summary of the main ideas and details in the corresponding area.

| Main idea | Main idea | Main idea |

Supporting details

Summary

39 Journalist Graphic Organizer

▶ Grades 5–12
▶ Social studies, English, science, health

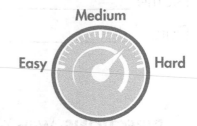

In their writing, journalists answer the five Ws: Who, What, Where, When, and Why. These questions are essential for writing and for reading text. By answering the five Ws, students will better comprehend texts and be able to articulate what they know and understand through their own writing.

Tips for Classroom Implementation

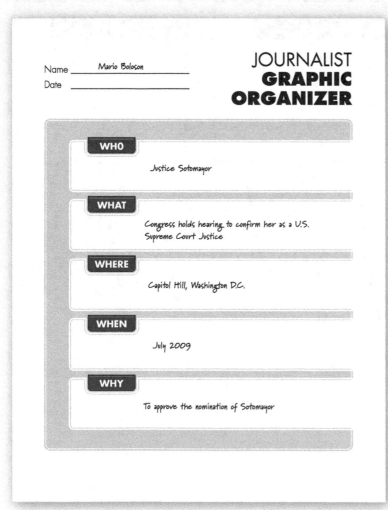

Name _____ Mario Boloson _____

Date _____

JOURNALIST GRAPHIC ORGANIZER

WHO
Justice Sotomayor

WHAT
Congress holds hearing to confirm her as a U.S. Supreme Court Justice

WHERE
Capitol Hill, Washington D.C.

WHEN
July 2009

WHY
To approve the nomination of Sotomayor

You will need to model this graphic organizer. After they have filled out the organizer, asking students the additional questions "What do you know now?" and "Why is it important?" fosters personal response and greater comprehension. I love to ask my students these two questions. I learn a great deal about their thinking and what I need to do next as their teacher. It is through reflection, as prompted by these two questions, that students are more likely to synthesize what they are learning.

Name _____

Date _____

JOURNALIST
GRAPHIC
ORGANIZER

WHO

WHAT

WHERE

WHEN

WHY

40 Story Board Notes: Three Frame

▶ Grades 5–12
▶ Social studies, English, science, health, mathematics

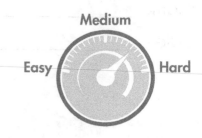

When students visually represent what they are learning, they increase their understanding and comprehension, and the Story Board graphic organizer facilitates this process. The boxes prompt the student to create visual images of an episode, event, or scene. Each box represents a scene, main event, step, or stage. The three-frame story board prompts students to focus on the beginning, middle, or end of a story or the situation, problem, and solution for a history lesson or science experiment, for example. These story frames are also applicable for problem solving in mathematics. The three boxes can present the problem, the approach to solving the problem, and then the final solution. The line in each box prompts students to use words to explain what they are portraying. This graphic organizer prompts students to think in both words and pictures. By identifying key information, students develop their skills in academic literacy and critical thinking. You can use it to assess the students' understanding of newly acquired material.

Tips for Classroom Implementation

You will need to model how to use this graphic organizer. Encourage students to put as much detail as possible into their visualizations.

Although story boards appear to be a simplistic activity, they aren't. We know that having students visually represent what they read helps them comprehend the text. We also know that when activities incorporate several intelligences, students have improved comprehension. Story Boards incorporate visual, kinesthetic, artistic, and, if the students are working in pairs or groups, social-emotional learning. I witnessed this in my own classroom as well as that of my friend Mary Green, who teaches seventh graders in Chicago. Mary's students were clearly developing their comprehension skills as we observed how the students' story boards contained an increasing amount of detail as they read novels in literature circles.

Name _____

Date _____

STORY BOARD
NOTES

Topic Story Board Notes: Three Frame

DIRECTIONS: For each box, write a short description of the scene and draw a picture for the scene.

41 Story Board Notes: Six Frame

See the description for graphic organizer 40, Story Board Notes: Three Frame.

Name _____ Susan Hopes _____

Date _____ 21-Oct-09 _____

STORY BOARD NOTES

Topic Story Board Notes: Six Frame

DIRECTIONS: For each box, write a short description of the scene and draw a picture for the scene.

Juliet Dove Queen of Love

When Juliet gets the amulet of love.

When she meets the rats.

She talks to Athena.

When she unlocks the amulet.

When Eris is being mean to her.

When Cupid is released.

Name _____

Date _____

Topic Story Board Notes: Six Frame

DIRECTIONS: For each box, write a short description of the scene and draw a picture for the scene.

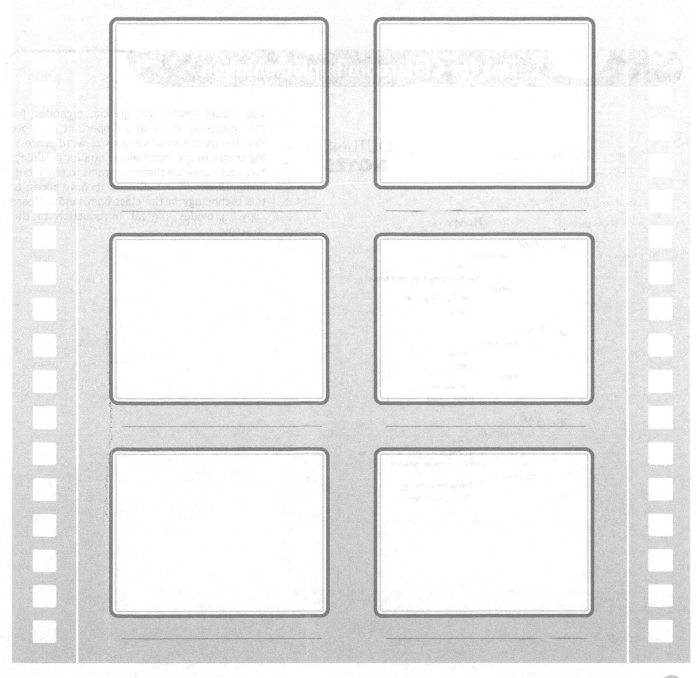

42   Outline Notes

▶ Grades 5—12
▶ Social studies, English, science, health, mathematics

I remember when I learned how to take notes in outline form during my freshman year of high school. Even today, I still take notes using this method of organization. Although a traditional strategy for taking notes, it is still quite helpful and an effective strategy for organizing information and generating ideas. Outline note taking is particularly effective with textbooks, as they are themselves structured in outline form.

Tips for Classroom Implementation

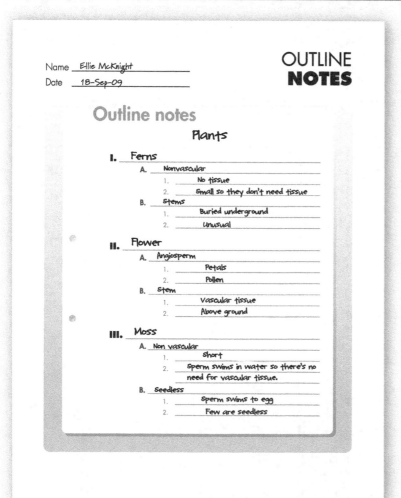

You should model this graphic organizer for the students. It is also important to note that the most recent versions of word processing programs are especially useful for outlining. You could draw on these programs to teach outlining. However, not all students have access to this technology in the classroom, and a "hard copy" provides a great introduction to this strategy.

Name _____

Date _____

Outline notes

I. _____

    A. _____

        1. _____

        2. _____

    B. _____

        1. _____

        2. _____

II. _____

    A. _____

        1. _____

        2. _____

    B. _____

        1. _____

        2. _____

III. _____

    A. _____

        1. _____

        2. _____

    B. _____

        1. _____

        2. _____

43 The Five Senses

▶ Grades 5—12
▶ Social studies, English, science, health

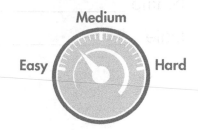

Medium

Easy   Hard

Using the five senses (sight, hearing, smell, taste, and touch) facilitates students' ability to identify and comprehend new information, as well as prompts them to extend what they know and understand about the information. Model this graphic organizer for students.

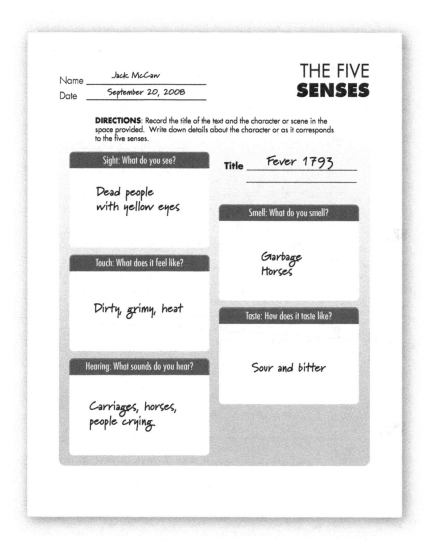

Name ___Jack McCaw___
Date ___September 20, 2008___

THE FIVE
SENSES

DIRECTIONS: Record the title of the text and the character or scene in the space provided. Write down details about the character or as it corresponds to the five senses.

Sight: What do you see?

Dead people with yellow eyes

Touch: What does it feel like?

Dirty, grimy, heat

Hearing: What sounds do you hear?

Carriages, horses, people crying

Title ___Fever 1793___

Smell: What do you smell?

Garbage
Horses

Taste: How does it taste like?

Sour and bitter

THE FIVE SENSES

Name _____

Date _____

DIRECTIONS: Record the title of the text and the character or scene in the space provided. Write down details about the character or as it corresponds to the five senses.

Sight: What do you see?

Title _____

_____

Smell: What do you smell?

Touch: What does it feel like?

Taste: How does it taste like?

Hearing: What sounds do you hear?

44　Cycle or Food Chain

▶ Grades 5–12
▶ Social studies, English, science, health, mathematics

This graphic organizer prompts students to identify important and critical information in a sequence. It is especially useful for creating a plot chart for a narrative text, illustrating a scientific sequence, identifying the steps to solve a math equation, or identifying important facts of an historical event. Model this graphic organizer for the students when you introduce it.

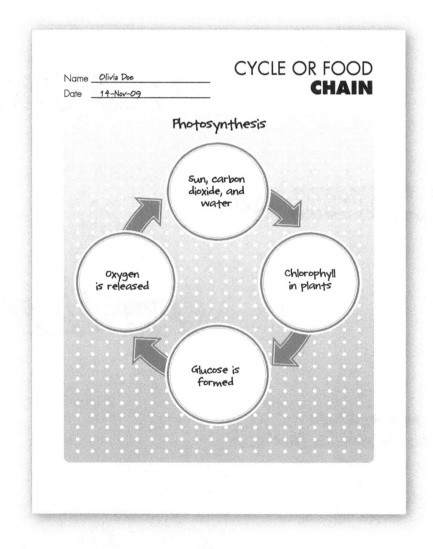

CYCLE OR FOOD
CHAIN

Name _____

Date _____

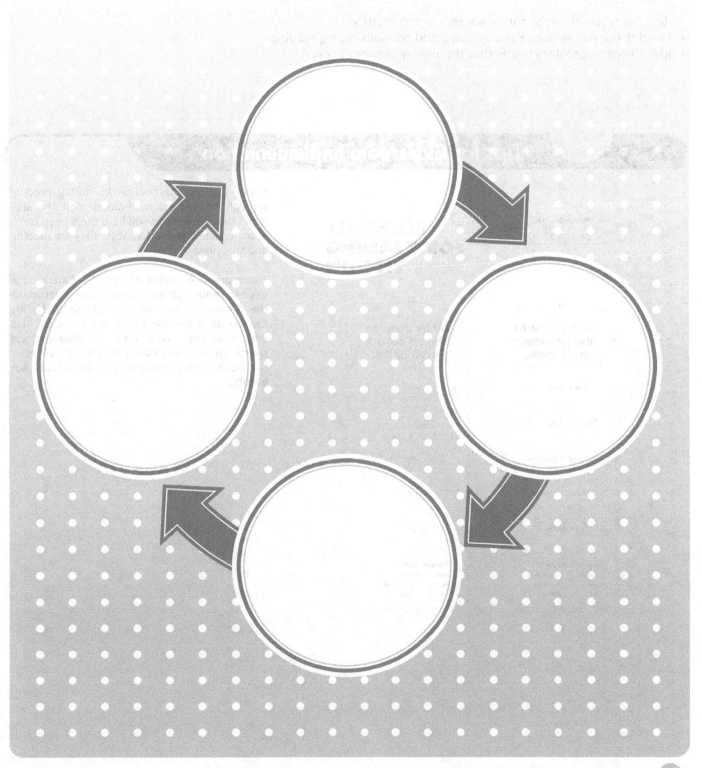

45–48 Bookmarks

▶ Grades 5—12
▶ Social studies, English, science

I have always found bookmarks to be one of the most helpful tools for active reading. They allow students to record important information while they are reading, and can be used for

- Keeping track of important characters or information
- Logging the reader's questions, ideas, and opinions during reading
- Identifying vocabulary words that the reader may not know

Tips for Classroom Implementation

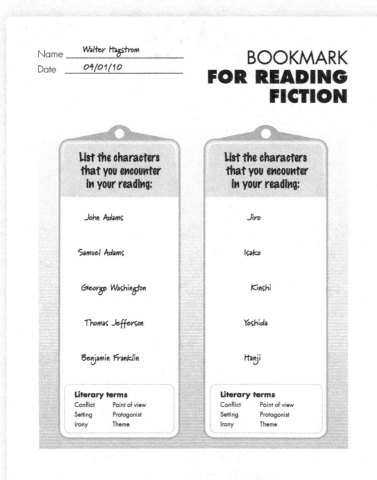

Model the use of bookmarks during reading through an in-class read-aloud. Tell the students that bookmarks will help them keep track of important information while they are reading and studying.

There are two copies of each bookmark on a page to reduce photocopying. I like to laminate the bookmarks for the students so that they can be used for the entire school year. Also encourage the students to use diagrams and charts on the bookmarks so that it is easier to visually track characters or important plot events.

Name _____

Date _____

BOOKMARK
FOR READING
FICTION

List the characters that you encounter in your reading:

Literary terms

Conflict	Point of view
Setting	Protagonist
Irony	Theme

List the characters that you encounter in your reading:

Literary terms

Conflict	Point of view
Setting	Protagonist
Irony	Theme

Name _____

Date _____

This bookmark reminds students of important strategies to use while they are reading.

Reading reminders

- Ask questions while you are reading.

- Make personal questions about what you're reading to your own experiences and what you know about the world.

- Preview and scan the text before you begin reading so that you have an idea about what the reading is about.

- Use a variety of strategies while you are reading.

After you read ask yourself these questions to determine how well you have read the text:

- Did you read for at least 20 minutes?

- Did you use a variety of strategies while you were reading?

- Did you ask questions while you were reading?

- Did you make personal connections with your reading?

- Did you understand what you read?

What questions do you have about the reading?

Reading reminders

- Ask questions while you are reading.

- Make personal questions about what you're reading to your own experiences and what you know about the world.

- Preview and scan the text before you begin reading so that you have an idea about what the reading is about.

- Use a variety of strategies while you are reading.

After you read ask yourself these questions to determine how well you have read the text:

- Did you read for at least 20 minutes?

- Did you use a variety of strategies while you were reading?

- Did you ask questions while you were reading?

- Did you make personal connections with your reading?

- Did you understand what you read?

What questions do you have about the reading?

Name _____

Date _____

BOOKMARK
FOR QUESTIONS
DURING READING

Questions during reading

- Why does the character ...

- The main character wants to ...

- The author's writing reminds me of ...

- I predict that _____ will happen.

- I was surprised by ...

- If I could ask the character or author a question, it would be ...

- The following quote

_____

_____

_____p._____

is interesting to me because ...

_____

_____

_____.

- The main conflict is ...

- I wonder why ...

Questions during reading

- Why does the character ...

- The main character wants to ...

- The author's writing reminds me of ...

- I predict that _____ will happen.

- I was surprised by ...

- If I could ask the character or author a question, it would be ...

- The following quote

_____

_____

_____p._____

is interesting to me because ...

_____

_____

_____.

- The main conflict is ...

- I wonder why ...

TEXTBOOK
REMINDERS
BOOKMARK

Textbook reminders bookmark

Look at the chapter or section that you are about to read. What kinds of documents and texts will you read (i.e. maps, charts, graphs, vocabulary...)?

What kind of information is in the pull-out sections and side bars?

Are there different colors or fonts in the text? Why?

Does the textbook use color to make specific information more clear?

Look at the graphics and photos. What information do these visuals reveal and represent?

Textbook reminders bookmark

Look at the chapter or section that you are about to read. What kinds of documents and texts will you read (i.e. maps, charts, graphs, vocabulary...)?

What kind of information is in the pull-out sections and side bars?

Are there different colors or fonts in the text? Why?

Does the textbook use color to make specific information more clear?

Look at the graphics and photos. What information do these visuals reveal and represent?

Graphic organizers 49–53 are tools that facilitate students' independent evaluation of their own progress and their monitoring of assignments and homework.

49 Individual Performance in a Cooperative Group

▶ Grades 5–12
▶ All subjects

This graphic organizer encourages students to reflect on their learning and evaluate their individual performance in a cooperative group. It draws attention to their role in the success of that group in completing an assigned task.

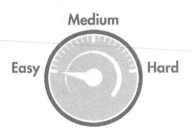
Easy — Medium — Hard

Tips for Classroom Implementation

Name ___Ruby McClain___

Date ___10/10/10___

COOPERATIVE GROUP

Topic Individual Performance in a Cooperative Group

DIRECTIONS: Look at the following categories and decide what description best represents your individual participation. Add the points for your total score.

	1	2	3	4	Your score
How did I work in my group?	I didn't focus on the group and the assigned work.	I sometimes listened to group members and sometimes paid attention.	I worked in my group and helped to get our work finished.	I worked in my group and helped get our work finished by helping other members and solved problems.	3
How prepared was I for my group?	I forgot to bring my work for the group.	I had my work and my materials most of the time.	I had my work and materials every time my group met.	I had my work and materials every time my group met and I helped other group members if they needed it.	3
How well did I cooperate in my group?	I didn't help my group members.	I sometimes helped my group members.	I shared my work and helped my group members if they asked.	I willingly shared my work and helped my group members.	4
How much did you help your group to solve problems?	I didn't help to solve problems.	I had some ideas but I didn't share them.	I had some ideas but didn't always share them.	I shared ideas and often asked my group members for suggestions and ideas to solve problems.	2
				Total	12

Working in groups often takes practice. The more students work in groups, they better they become at working with their peers. Honestly evaluating peers is particularly challenging. As the students consider the role that their classmates played in their group, they also reflect on their individual performance. When students reflect on their own work, they are more likely to internalize new skills and information. Discovering how each student can individually contribute or detract from a group's task is essential for successful collaborative learning experiences.

Name _____

Date _____

COOPERATIVE GROUP

Topic Individual Performance in a Cooperative Group

DIRECTIONS: Look at the following categories and decide what description best represents your individual participation. Add the points for your total score.

	1	2	3	4	Your score
How did I work in my group?	I didn't focus on the group and the assigned work.	I sometimes listened to group members and sometimes paid attention.	I worked in my group and helped to get our work finished.	I worked in my group and helped get our work finished by helping other members and solved problems.	
How prepared was I for my group?	I forgot to bring my work for the group.	I had my work and my materials most of the time.	I had my work and materials every time my group met.	I had my work and materials every time my group met and I helped other group members If they needed it.	
How well did I cooperate in my group?	I didn't help my group members.	I sometimes helped my group members.	I shared my work and helped my group members if they asked.	I willingly shared my work and helped my group members.	
How much did you help your group to solve problems?	I didn't help to solve problems.	I had some ideas but I didn't share them.	I had some ideas but didn't always share them.	I shared ideas and often asked my group members for suggestions and ideas to solve problems.	
				Total	

50 Cooperative Group Planner

▶ Grades 5—12
▶ All subjects

This organizer helps students plan the activities and jobs of individual members of a group. It is used to describe the activities and expectations for each group member.

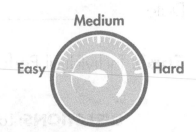

Medium

Easy · Hard

Tips for Classroom Implementation

Name *Olivia Doe*
Date *14-Nov-09*

COOPERATIVE GROUP PLANNER

Topic Cooperative Group Work Planner

DIRECTIONS: Use this planner to help you and your fellow group members work collaboratively on the assignment/project.

1. Does everyone know each other? Write down the names of your group members and one thing that you know about them.

   Jim likes baseball and his favorite subject is math. Katie is on the swim team and likes to read historical books. Ellie is in the school play and likes English class. Colin plays the guitar and likes art.

2. Groups work well together when they have strategies for talking about ideas and material. Write down at least two strategies that your group will use in your discussions.

   Everyone will contribute to discussions by taking turns. Once someone speaks, they can't speak again until all of the other group members have contributed.
   If you have an idea that you would like to add, write it down on an index card. We will put up all of the index cards and ideas and then choose which ones we will use.

3. Be positive. List some ways in which you will contribute to a positive group dynamic.

   We promise to not make mean comments about each other. We also promise to bring our work in on time and make sure that it is completed. When a group member does a good job, we will make sure to mention it.

4. Assigning tasks. Groups work better when individual members have assigned tasks to complete. What will each group member do for this project?

   Since Jim and Colin are good at technology, they will work together to create the power point for the presentation. Katie is a good writer so she will edit our writing and put it together for the powerpoint. Ellie is good at speaking so she will be the main narrator for the powerpoint.

How many times have we heard our students say, "Well _____ (insert name) was supposed to do that?" When a collaborative assignment is due, oftentimes unsuccessful groups begin to blame each other. I believe that the source of most of the students' lack of success comes from poor planning. This cooperative group planner, prompts students to organize the tasks and goals for the group. If the students write down the plan for the cooperative group activity, it is been my experience that the blame game dissipates. Writing down the plan is akin to a contract and the students maintain a stronger commitment to the work. Teachers can also use the cooperative group planner to monitor the students' initial organization of the group's work.

Name _____

Date _____

COOPERATIVE GROUP
PLANNER

Topic Cooperative Group Work Planner

DIRECTIONS: Use this planner to help you and your fellow group members work collaboratively on the assignment/project.

1. Does everyone know each other? Write down the names of your group members and one thing that you know about them.

2. Groups work well together when they have strategies for talking about ideas and material. Write down at least two strategies that your group will use in your discussions.

3. Be positive. List some ways in which you will contribute to a positive group dynamic.

4. Assigning tasks. Groups work better when individual members have assigned tasks to complete. What will each group member do for this project?

51 Portfolio Tracker

▶ Grades 5–12
▶ All subjects

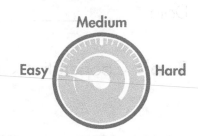

Portfolios are a collection of student work. Designed to demonstrate students' development of knowledge and skills, they can be a substantive and rewarding form of assessment. In order for portfolio assessment to be effective, students must actively participate in keeping track of their portfolio contents.

Tips for Classroom Implementation

Name _____ Paul Plates _____
Date _____ 21-Apr-09 _____

PORTFOLIO TRACKER

PORTFOLIO TRACKER

DIRECTIONS: Use this form to log the contents of your portfolio. Attach this to your portfolio.

Completion date	Title of work	Why was this work selected?
Nov. 16th.	My neighborhood map	I did a good job on this and it was fine.
Feb. 3rd.	Ancient Egyptian test	I learned a lot and even though I did poorly on it I learned a lot.
Mar. 19th.	Latin America video worksheet	The video was well done and I learned a lot.
Dec. 5th.	Europe map project	I learned about all of the countries in Europe.
Oct. 31st.	Africa powerpoint	I learned the different types of governments in Africa.

When you introduce portfolios to your students, explain that they document their journeys as learners. The portfolios should contain examples of their best work and examples that demonstrate their journeys. Both you and the individual student should determine what to include in the portfolio.

Name _____

Date _____

PORTFOLIO TRACKER

DIRECTIONS: Use this form to log the contents of your portfolio.
Attach this to your portfolio.

Completion date	Title of work	Why was this work selected?

52 Independent Reading Log

▶ Grades 5–12
▶ All subjects

Reading books independently is integral to students' literacy development. A reading log is a place for students to record their reading selections. It also assists students in identifying patterns—for example, preferred genres or authors.

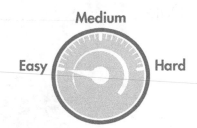

Tips for Classroom Implementation

Name ___Julie Flecher___

Date ___11–Feb–09___

INDEPENDENT READING LOG

PORTFOLIO TRACKER

DIRECTIONS: Each time that you finish a book, record the information in this independent reading log.

Date	Title and author	Comments	Genre (realistic fiction, comedy, fantasy, mystery, biography, poetry, adventure, nonfiction, science fiction, reference, folk or fairy tale)
3/14/09	Juliet Dove, Queen of love by Bruce coville	It was really good and it held my attention through the whole book.	Fantasy
4/06/09	Percy Jackson and the Olympians. The Last Olympian by Rick Riordan	It was fun to read and had a lot of action.	Fantasy
5/19/09	Twilight by Stephanie Meyer	It had action, romance, and holds your attentiion.	Fantasy
6/12/09	My 30 Years Backstairs at the White House by Lillian Rogers parks	This book reminds you of the little people that kept American going.	Biography
7/9/09	Harry Potter and the Deathly Hallows	This book kept you reading and it was filled with action.	Fantasy

Introduce the reading log to the students and explain that they are to record the author, title, and genre of the book, and to include comments. Explain to the students that in the comments section they are to write down any questions they might have about the book, discuss what was interesting and what they liked about the book, and whether or not they would recommend the book.

Name _____

Date _____

INDEPENDENT
READING LOG

PORTFOLIO TRACKER

DIRECTIONS: Each time that you finish a book, record the information in this independent reading log.

Date	Title and author	Comments	Genre (realistic fiction, comedy, fantasy, mystery, biography, poetry, adventure, nonfiction, science fiction, reference, folk or fairy tale)

53 Assignment Tracker

▶ Grades 5–12
▶ All subjects

Staying organized and keeping track of assignments are integral to student success. Through regular use of the assignment tracker, students can develop a sense of control of their academic work.

Tips for Classroom Implementation

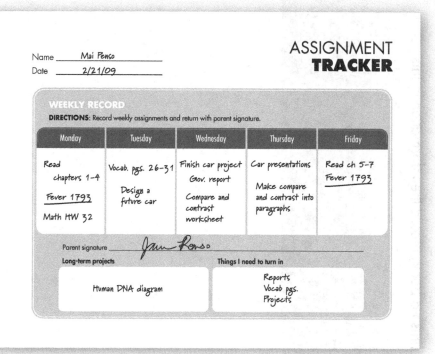

Allow students to take some time on Mondays to complete the assignment tracker. Remind them of due dates for the weekly assignments. The requirement of a parent signature can remind the students to communicate with their parents about assignments. The parents can also help in monitoring the completion of assignments.

ASSIGNMENT TRACKER

Name _____

Date _____

WEEKLY RECORD

DIRECTIONS: Record weekly assignments and return with parent signature.

Monday	Tuesday	Wednesday	Thursday	Friday

Parent signature _____

Things I need to turn in

Long-term projects

CHAPTER FIVE

Graphic Organizers for Supporting Reading Comprehension

This chapter focuses on graphic organizers and reading strategies that support students' reading comprehension. As we know, effective readers use a wide variety of strategies that include

- Previewing
- Setting a purpose
- Connecting
- Using prior knowledge

- Predicting
- Visualizing
- Monitoring
- Making inferences

Each graphic organizer and strategy in this chapter will refer to this list of successful reading strategies.

54 Questioning the Author

▶ Grades 5—12
▶ Social studies, English, science

Students will develop the following reading strategies:

• Connecting
• Using prior knowledge
• Predicting
• Making inferences

This is a strategy in which students use a series of questions to determine the author's purpose and the extent to which the author was successful; through these questions, the students must make an effort to fully comprehend the text. This strategy was originally developed by McKeown, Beck, and Worthy (1993).

Tips for Classroom Implementation

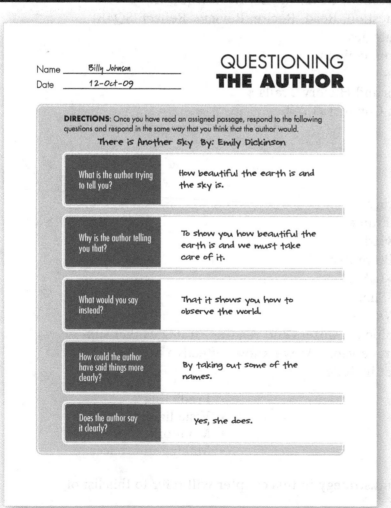

This is a challenging content reading strategy and one of the most important. It has been my experience that when students question the author and take on a different point of view or perspective, they begin to develop more complex and deeper comprehension of text.

The Directed Reading and Thinking Activity develops the students purpose for reading a selected text. This activity helps students to become more active readers as questions are considered during their reading. When students use this activity, especially when they are reading textbooks, they are better able to focus on the content and main ideas and concepts.

QUESTIONING
THE AUTHOR

Name _____

Date _____

DIRECTIONS: Once you have read an assigned passage, respond to the following questions and respond in the same way that you think that the author would.

What is the author trying to tell you?

Why is the author telling you that?

What would you say instead?

How could the author have said things more clearly?

Does the author say it clearly?

55 Question-Answer-Relationship (QAR)

▶ Grades 5—12
▶ Social studies, English, science

Students will develop the following reading strategies:

- Connecting
- Using prior knowledge
- Predicting

- Visualizing
- Monitoring
- Making inferences

This reading strategy, developed by Taffy Raphael (1982), requires students to create questions of specific types, enabling them to become more strategic in their comprehension because they will understand where the information that is needed to answer the question will come from.

Tips for Classroom Implementation

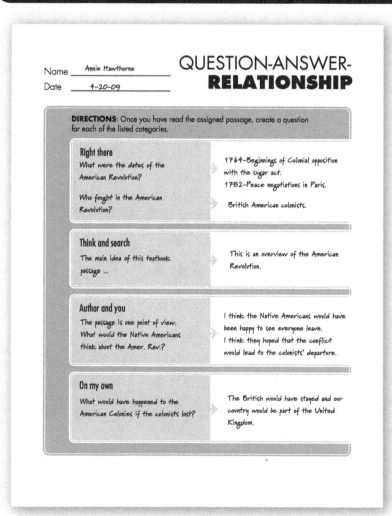

Name Annie Hawthorne
Date 4-20-09

QUESTION-ANSWER-
RELATIONSHIP

DIRECTIONS: Once you have read the assigned passage, create a question for each of the listed categories.

Right there
What were the dates of the American Revolution?

Who fought in the American Revolution?

1764-Beginnings of Colonial opposition with the sugar act.
1782-Peace negotiations in Paris.

British American colonists.

Think and search
The main idea of this textbook passage ...

This is an overview of the American Revolution.

Author and you
The passage is one point of view. What would the Native Americans think about the Amer. Rev.?

I think the Native Americans would have been happy to see everyone leave.
I think they hoped that the conflict would lead to the colonists' departure.

On my own
What would have happened to the American Colonies if the colonists lost?

The British would have stayed and our country would be part of the United Kingdom.

This is one of the most challenging content reading strategies. Begin teaching this strategy by helping students understand that their questions will come from the text or their previous knowledge. Raphael refers to these as the core categories: In the Book and In My Head.

As the students become proficient with these two categories, Raphael suggests that the students move to the next level of comprehension question. In the Book becomes the two organizer sections Right There and Think and Search. The In My Head category becomes the sections Author and You and On My Own.

Be sure to explain the different kinds of questions:

Right There. The answer is in the text.
Think and Search. The answer is in the text, but you might have to look in several different sentences to find it.
Author and You. The answer is not in the text. However, you will use information from the text and what you may already know to respond to this type of question.
On My Own. The answer is not in the text. The answer comes from you.

I often found that my students had the most difficult differentiating between the Author and You and On My Own sections. Give the students many examples and model questions that you, as a reader, would create for those sections.

QUESTION-ANSWER-
RELATIONSHIP

Name _____

Date _____

DIRECTIONS: Once you have read the assigned passage, create a question for each of the listed categories.

Right there

Think and search

Author and you

On my own

56 Gist

▶ Grades 5–12
▶ Social studies, English, science

Students will develop the following reading strategies:

- Monitoring
- Making inferences

The students will also develop their ability to summarize text.

Tips for Classroom Implementation

Name ___Marvin Phelps___   **GIST**

Date ___12-Feb-09___

Title of reading selection ___Nefertiti___

DIRECTIONS: Preview the reading selection and write down the keywords and phrases in the space, *Keywords and phrases*.

Write a 20-word sentence summary using as many of the keywords as you can.

> **Keywords and phrases**
>
> Nefertiti was the great royal wife of Akhenaten, an Egyptian Pharaoh.
>
> • She and her husband believed in the God, Aten.
> • She is famous for her beauty.

20-word sentence summary

Nefertiti	was	the	wife
of	Akhenaten	a	Pharaoh
She	believed	in	Aten
the	sun	God	she
also	was	a	bust

Follow these directions when teaching the gist strategy and accompanying graphic organizer.

1. Students will preview the text, paying particular attention to headings, subheadings, and bolded vocabulary.
2. Both you and the students will create a first draft outline using an overhead projector, chalkboard, or LCD computer projector.
3. The students will read the text and use the outline as a guide for understanding the text.
4. When the students complete their reading, they will create main idea statements and add important details. You should provide guidance and modeling for this step.
5. The students will create a summarizing statement for the entire text passage. They must use the exact number of words as prompted in the graphic organizer.

My students positively responded to this strategy. There is a competitive element in that the students had to create a summary with the exact number of required words.

Name _____

Date _____

GIST

Title of reading selection _____

DIRECTIONS: Preview the reading selection and write down the key words and phrases in the space, *Key words and phrases.*

Write a 20-word sentence summary using as many of the key words as you can.

Key words and phrases

20-word sentence summary

_____ _____

_____ _____

_____ _____

_____ _____

_____ _____

57 Survey, Question, Read, Recite, Review (SQ3R)

▶ Grades 5–12
▶ Social studies, English, science

SQ3R is effective in supporting students in developing independent strategic reading skills.

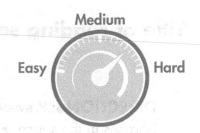

Students will develop the following reading strategies:

- Previewing
- Setting a purpose
- Connecting
- Using prior knowledge

- Predicting
- Monitoring
- Making inferences

Tips for Classroom Implementation

Name _____ Erik Watterton _____

Date _____ 30-Jan-09 _____

SQ3R

Title Survey, Question, Read, Recite, Review (cont'd)
Topic _____ Causes of the American Revolusion _____

SURVEY Look at the headings and vocabulary. Make some predictions about what you will learn.

> I will learn about the causes and the effects of the American Revolution. There were also a lot of legislative acts that provoked the colonists to rebel against British rule.

Take the headings and turn them into questions. Also write down vocabulary words.

Questions and vocabulary	Answers
What were the different acts?	Sugar Act, Townshend Act, Quartering Act.
What act was the worst one to the colonists?	The Quartering Act was the worst because the colonists had to give housing and food to British soldiers.
What event started the fighting?	Maybe the Boston Tea Party. There were actually several things that started the fighting.
How did the revolution finally end?	The peace talks in Paris.

READ the text and write down the answers to your questions.

RECITE and check your answers with a partner.

Explain the steps that students are to follow when using the SQ3R graphic organizer:

1. **Survey.** Survey the chapter prior to reading. Look at the headings and subheadings, and skim the introduction and conclusion.
2. **Question.** Once you have identified the headings, turn them into questions.
3. **Read.** Read the selection and work on answering the created questions.
4. **Recite.** Once you have completed the reading, close the text and orally summarize what you just read. You should take notes in your own words.
5. **Review.** Study the notes and use them to remember what the reading was about.

The students will need numerous opportunities to practice this strategy in order to become more active and independent.

Name _____

Date _____

SQ3R

Title Survey, Question, Read, Recite, Review (cont'd)

Topic _____

SURVEY Look at the headings and vocabulary. Make some predictions about what you will learn.

[ ]

Take the headings and turn them into questions. Also write down vocabulary words.

Questions and vocabulary	Answers

READ the text and write down the answers to your questions.

RECITE and check your answers with a partner.

Name _____

Date _____

SQ3R

Title Survey, Question, Read, Recite, Review (cont'd)

SUMMARY

Write a short summary of the text.

The textbook section provides an overview of the event and legislative acts that the British imposed on the American colonists. There were several years of these kinds of events and it took some time for the American colonists to get annoyed enough to go to war. Not all of the colonists fought in the revolution. There were Tories. These were American colonists who were loyal to the British government and didn't want a revolution.

REVIEW the answers to the questions and the vocabulary word definitions with a classmate.

I didn't know what a Tory was when I started to read the passage. I also learned about the Townshend Acts and what quartering means.

Name _____

Date _____

Title Survey, Question, Read, Recite, Review (cont'd)

SUMMARY
Write a short summary of the text.

REVIEW the answers to the questions and the vocabulary word definitions with a classmate.

58 Survey, Question, Read, Recite, Review, Reflect (SQ4R)

▶ Grades 5–12
▶ Social studies, English, science

Similar to SQ3R, this organizer has an additional step that supports students in reading text strategically.

Students will develop the following reading strategies:

- Previewing
- Setting a purpose
- Connecting
- Using prior knowledge

- Predicting
- Monitoring
- Making inferences

Tips for Classroom Implementation

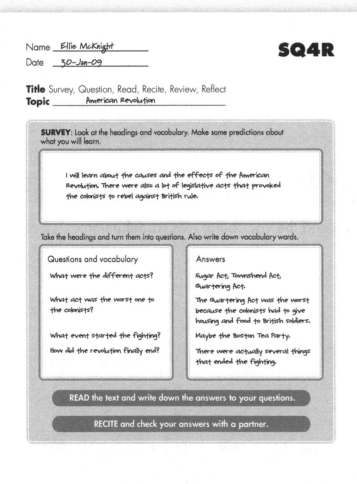

Name Ellie McKnight

Date 30-Jan-09

SQ4R

Title Survey, Question, Read, Recite, Review, Reflect
Topic _____ American Revolution _____

SURVEY: Look at the headings and vocabulary. Make some predictions about what you will learn.

> I will learn about the causes and the effects of the American Revolution. There were also a lot of legislative acts that provoked the colonists to rebel against British rule.

Take the headings and turn them into questions. Also write down vocabulary words.

Questions and vocabulary	Answers
What were the different acts?	Sugar Act, Townshend Act, Quartering Act.
What act was the worst one to the colonists?	The Quartering Act was the worst because the colonists had to give housing and food to British soldiers.
What event started the fighting?	Maybe the Boston Tea Party.
How did the revolution finally end?	There were actually several things that ended the fighting.

READ the text and write down the answers to your questions.

RECITE and check your answers with a partner.

Explain the steps that students are to follow when using the SQ4R graphic organizer:

1. **Survey.** Survey the chapter prior to reading. Look at the headings and subheadings, and skim the introduction and conclusion.
2. **Question.** Once you have identified the headings, turn them into questions.
3. **Read.** Read the selection and work on answering the created questions.
4. **Recite.** Once you have completed the reading, close the text and orally summarize what you just read. You should take notes in your own words.
5. **Review.** Study the notes and use them to remember what the reading was about.
6. **Reflect.** Write down what this information means to you and how it contributes to your understanding of the text.

As with SQ3R, students will need numerous opportunities to practice this strategy in order to become more active and independent.

Name _____

Date _____

SQ4R

Title Survey, Question, Read, Recite, Review, Reflect
Topic _____

SURVEY: Look at the headings and vocabulary. Make some predictions about what you will learn.

Take the headings and turn them into questions. Also write down vocabulary words.

Questions and vocabulary

Answers

READ the text and write down the answers to your questions.

RECITE and check your answers with a partner.

Name _____

Date _____

SQ4R

Title Survey, Question, Read, Recite, Review, Reflect (cont'd)

SUMMARY

Write a short summary of the text.

The textbook section provides an overview of the event and legislative acts that the British imposed on the American Colonists. There were several years of these kinds of events and it took some time for the American colonists to get annoyed enough to go to war. Not all of the colonists fought in the revolution. There were Tories. These were American colonists who were loyal to the British government and didn't want a revolution.

REVIEW the answers to the questions and the vocabulary word definitions with a classmate.

I didn't know what a Tory was when I started to read the passage, I also learned about the Townsend Acts and what quartering means.

REFLECT

What did you learn about the topic and why is this important?

I learned that the American Revolution was caused by several events over many years. It took a lot for the American colonists to get angry and frustrated enough to start to rebel. This is important because these kinds of historical conflicts are actually pretty complex. Sometimes when I learn about these sorts of things in history, I just think that it might have been just one event that caused a war. It is actually much more complex.

Name _____

Date _____

Title Survey, Question, Read, Recite, Review, Reflect (cont'd)

SUMMARY
Write a short summary of the text.

REVIEW the answers to the questions and the vocabulary word definitions with a classmate.

REFLECT
What did you learn about the topic and why is this important?

59 Fix-Up Strategies

▶ Grades 5–12
▶ All subjects

As students read, they may run into difficulty comprehending a text. This graphic organizer reminds students of key strategies that can help them understand text when they are struggling.

Tips for Classroom Implementation

Explain each of the fix-up strategies and model it for your students. You and your students can also add strategies. The students can create a bookmark with these strategies or paste them inside their notebooks for an easily accessible reference.

Name ____Eric Stiles____

Date ____12/15/10____

FIX-UP STRATEGIES

PREVIEW
Get a sense of a text before reading.

I think this book is about teenage boys in gangs.

PREDICT
Guess what will happen.

They'll fight with the other boys and win.

SET A PURPOSE
Decide why you are reading.

For fun.
To learn more about high school kids.

VISUALIZE
Create a mental picture.

A bunch of boys, greased hair, standing around a cool old car.

CONNECT
Relate personally to what you read.

Ponyboy reminds me of my cousin, Ben.
Johnny is like my friend, Tony.

MONITOR
Check your comprehension as you read.

USE PRIOR KNOWLEDGE
Think of what you already know about the topic.

Boys in gangs usually have bad home lives.

MAKE INFERENCES
Develop logical guesses based on the text and your own experiences.

I bet Cherry will switch gangs to be with the greasers.

Name _____

Date _____

FIX-UP
STRATEGIES

PREVIEW
Get a sense of a text before reading.

PREDICT
Guess what will happen.

SET A PURPOSE
Decide why you are reading.

VISUALIZE
Create a mental picture.

CONNECT
Relate personally to what you read.

MONITOR
Check your comprehension as you read.

USE PRIOR KNOWLEDGE
Think of what you already know about the topic.

MAKE INFERENCES
Develop logical guesses based on the text and your own experiences.

60 Reading Connections

▶ Grades 5–12
▶ All subjects

Students will develop the following reading strategies:

- Connecting
- Using prior knowledge
- Monitoring
- Making inferences

When students connect to a text, they are personally responding to it. This organizer prompts students to make four types of personal connections: to personal experiences, current events and prior knowledge, other subjects, and other texts.

Tips for Classroom Implementation

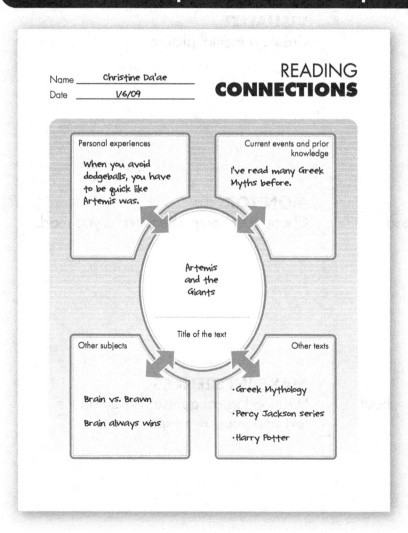

Be sure to explain to the students that the personal connections they make during their reading will help them with their understanding of the text. Discuss the four types of personal connections that we can make with texts. Remember, effective and successful readers make connections both to their personal lives and to the "real world."

READING
CONNECTIONS

Name _____

Date _____

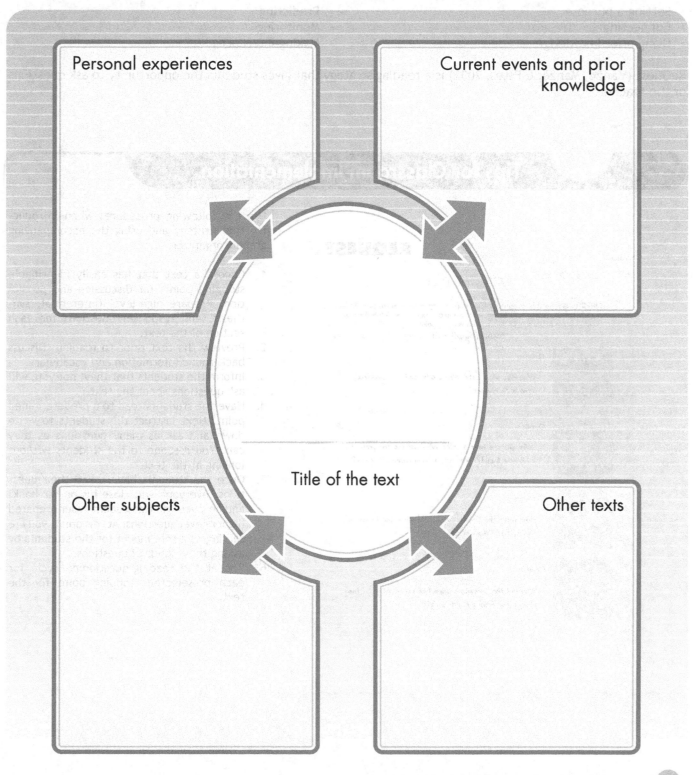

Personal experiences

Current events and prior knowledge

Title of the text

Other subjects

Other texts

61 ReQuest

▶ Grades 5–12
▶ All subjects

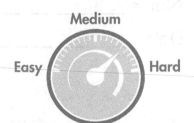

Students will develop the following reading strategies:

- Setting a purpose
- Connecting
- Using prior knowledge

- Predicting
- Monitoring
- Making inferences

ReQuest (Manzo, Manzo, & Estes, 2001) is a reading strategy that gives students the opportunity to ask questions of the teacher.

Tips for Classroom Implementation

REQUEST

Name _____ Helen _____
Date _____ 12-Oct-09 _____

ReQuest

DIRECTIONS: Read the assigned text and stop reading as requested by your teacher. At each stopping point, you will create questions to ask your teacher. Write down as many questions as you can. Do this for each stopping point.

Bastet (Egyptian Goddess)

Stopping point 1
Questions
Why was she a cat? Why a solar and war Goddess? Who is Sekhment?

Stopping point 2
Questions
Why did she have a cult? Why was she the protector of lower Egypt? Why was a town named after her?

Stopping point 3
Questions
Who were the 2 solar Gods? Why was she known as eye of Ra? Who was God of fire?

Stopping point 4
Questions
Why did the Greeks change her name? Why did they change her from a lion to a cat?

Use the following procedures when introducing this strategy and using the accompanying graphic organizer.

1. Choose a text that has easily identifiable stopping points for discussion and prediction. Prepare high-level (inferential, synthesis, and response) questions for each section of the text.
2. Preview the text prior to reading. Discuss background information and vocabulary.
3. Inform the students that they, not you, will ask questions about the text.
4. Have the students read to a predetermined point. Next instruct the students to write down and ask as many questions as they can. You respond to the students *without* looking at the text.
5. Once the students have asked their questions, everyone will close his or her book, and now you will ask students your prepared higher-level questions. At this point, you are serving as a role model for the students by asking these kinds of questions.
6. Repeat the reading-questioning cycle for each preselected stopping point for the text.

REQUEST

Name _____

Date _____

DIRECTIONS: Read the assigned text and stop reading as requested by your teacher. At each stopping point, you will create questions to ask your teacher. Write down as many questions as you can. Do this for each stopping point.

Stopping point 1

Questions _____
_____
_____
_____

Stopping point 2

Questions _____
_____
_____
_____

Stopping point 3

Questions _____
_____
_____
_____

Stopping point 4

Questions _____
_____
_____
_____

62   Story Trails and History Trails

▶ Grades 5–12
▶ All subjects

Medium

Easy   Hard

Students will develop the following reading strategies:

- Connecting
- Using prior knowledge
- Predicting

- Visualizing
- Making inferences

This graphic organizer offers a structure for students to put events from a story or the stages of an historical event into chronological order. An understanding of the key events facilitates greater exploration into the structure of the story.

Are the events related by cause and effect, do they connect as situation-problem-solution, or is the story simply one of beginning-middle-end? Recording the text and visual images of the key events also enhances students' comprehension.

Tips for Classroom Implementation

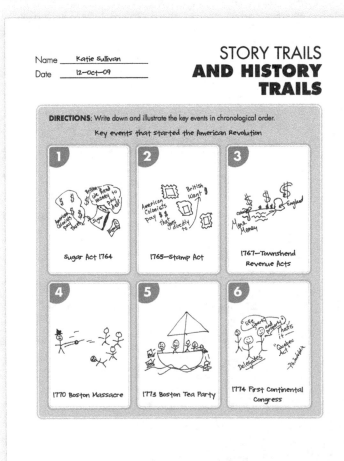

When you first introduce students to story trails, select the key events through a large group discussion. As the students recall the events, arrange them in chronological order and instruct the students to reexamine these events for specific details that can be illustrated.

Name _____

Date _____

STORY TRAILS
AND HISTORY
TRAILS

DIRECTIONS: Write down and illustrate the key events in chronological order.

1

2

3

4

5

6

63 Text-Think-Connect (TTC)

▶ Grades 5–12
▶ Social studies, English, science

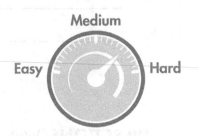

Students will develop the following reading strategies:

- Connecting
- Using prior knowledge
- Predicting
- Monitoring
- Making inferences

This reading tool graphically represents the student's response to learning.

Tips for Classroom Implementation

Name __Sarah Smith__

Date __1-Dec-09__

TTC

Topic Text, Think, Connect (TTC)

DIRECTIONS: Use this graphic organizer to record information from your reading and how this information connects to your personal experiences.

"Newts"

Text facts	What do you think about the text?	Connections How does this information connect to what you already know?
Amphibian in the Salamandridae family found in North America Europe, and Asia. They have 3 distinct developmental life stages lizard-like bodies, either fully aquatic or semi-aquatic.	It was a very informative article about newts and about what they are.	It connects by-I knew that they can live on land or water, and they live all over the world.

Explain the three columns of the graphic organizer and their purpose.

Text facts. In this column, students record important information. This information could include direct quotes or words and phrases that interest the reader.

What do you think about the text? In this column, students record what they think about the text and the author's message. The students should record their impressions and make efforts to interpret the text.

Connections. When we read, we make personal connections with the text. We connect the text to our personal experiences, knowledge, and beliefs. In this column, students record what this text reminds them of in their personal lives.

Name _____

Date _____

Topic Text, Think, Connect (TTC)

DIRECTIONS: Use this graphic organizer to record information from your reading and how this information connects to your personal experiences.

Text facts	What do you think about the text?	Connections How does this information connect to what you already know?

64 REAP

▶ Grades 5—12
▶ Social studies, English, science, mathematics, and health

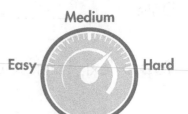

Students will develop the following reading strategies:

- Connecting
- Using prior knowledge
- Predicting

- Monitoring
- Making inferences
- Point of view

This hierarchical strategy is similar to Gist. REAP is an acronym for

Read the text.
Encode into your own language.
Annotate by writing the message. (The annotations can be personal connections, questions, notes, or a personal reaction to the text.)
Ponder the meaning of the text.

Tips for Classroom Implementation

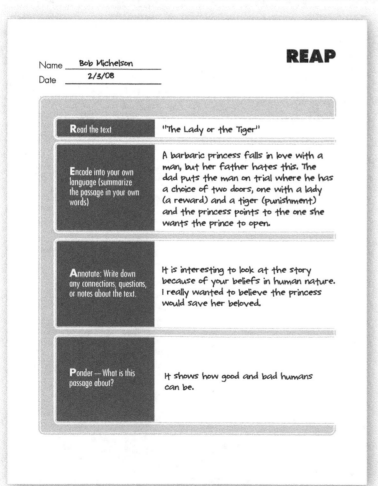

Writing effective summaries and notes takes practice. Students should have several opportunities to develop this skill.

REAP

Name _____

Date _____

Read the text

Encode into your own language (summarize the passage in your own words)

Annotate: Write down any connections, questions, or notes about the text.

Ponder—What is this passage about?

65 PLAN

▶ Grades 5–12
▶ Social studies, English, science

Students will develop the following reading strategies:

- Previewing
- Setting a purpose
- Connecting
- Using prior knowledge

- Predicting
- Monitoring
- Making inferences

PLAN is an acronym for *predict, locate, add,* and *note.* The PLAN strategy and accompanying graphic organizer help students visualize their reading.

Tips for Classroom Implementation

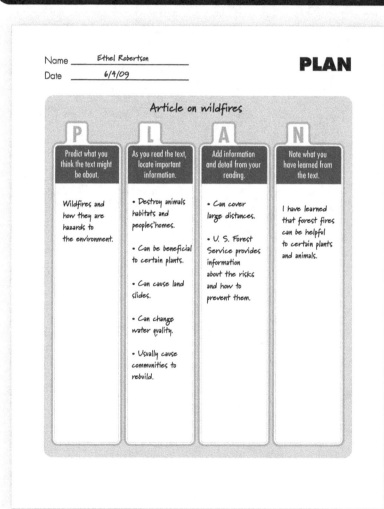

Name _____Ethel Robertson_____

Date _____6/4/09_____

PLAN

Article on wildfires

P — Predict what you think the text might be about.

Wildfires and how they are hazards to the environment.

L — As you read the text, locate important information.

- Destroy animals habitats and peoples' homes.
- Can be beneficial to certain plants.
- Can cause land slides.
- Can change water quality.
- Usually cause communities to rebuild.

A — Add information and detail from your reading.

- Can cover large distances.
- U. S. Forest Service provides information about the risks and how to prevent them.

N — Note what you have learned from the text.

I have learned that forest fires can be helpful to certain plants and animals.

Discuss the following directions and model the strategy for the students using a think-aloud.

Predict what you might learn from reading the text.

Locate important information as you read, using the following code: (?) for questions about the reading and (+) for what you think you learned from the text.

Add details and information to the graphic organizer from your reading.

Note and reflect on what you've learned.

Name _____

Date _____

PLAN

P	**L**	**A**	**N**
Predict what you think the text might be about.	As you read the text, locate important information.	Add information and detail from your reading.	Note what you have learned from the text.

66 PACA

▶ Grades 5–12
▶ Social studies, English, science

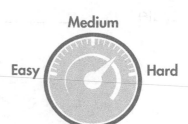

Students will develop the following reading strategies:

- Previewing
- Setting a purpose
- Connecting
- Using prior knowledge

- Predicting
- Monitoring
- Making inferences

PACA stands for *predicting and confirming activity*. Active readers make predictions as they read a text. This strategy prompts students to make predictions and seek confirmation in the text.

Tips for Classroom Implementation

Name _____ Marco Jolien _____

Date _____ Nov. 5, 2008 _____

PACA

Topic Predicting And Confirming Activity

"Mars, Meet Life"

Prediction	(+) if prediction is confirmed (−) if prediction is not confirmed	Support
Complicated for humans	+	Take 2 years to get to Mars, very cold (−60°c)
May be able to live there	+	Can make it warmer
Science is coming up with improvements	+	Use solar-powered engines (saves $)
Many problems	+	No water; only ice.
Some solutions	+	Release the carbon dioxide to create greenhouse effect = warmer

When you introduce this strategy, have the students predict what they might learn from the text. Students should think about what they already know and record that information on the PACA organizer.

Next, the students should read the text and confirm their predictions. If the prediction is confirmed, they should mark it with an (+); if the prediction is not confirmed, they should use a (−) sign. Students also record the text that supports their prediction.

Name _____

Date _____

Topic Predicting And Confirming Activity

Prediction	(+) if prediction is confirmed (−) if prediction is not confirmed	Support

67 DRTA

▶ Grades 5–12
▶ Social studies, English, science, health

Students will develop the following reading strategies:

- Previewing
- Setting a purpose
- Connecting
- Using prior knowledge

- Predicting
- Monitoring
- Making inferences

DRTA stands for *directed reading and thinking activity*. This organizer prompts students to preview the text and make predictions. As the students read the text, they should take notes that can provide support and evidence for their predictions.

Tips for Classroom Implementation

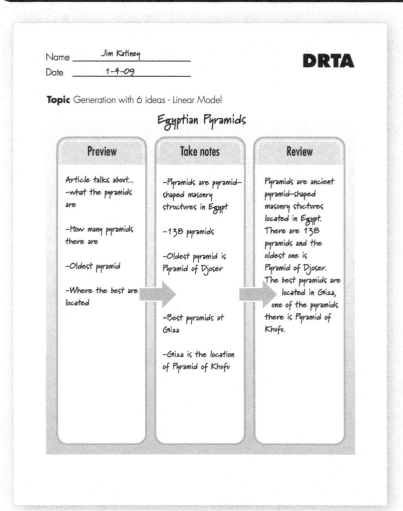

It is helpful to conduct a think-aloud and model the strategy before the students use the organizer independently.

Name _____

Date _____

DRTA

Topic Generation with 6 Ideas – Linear Model

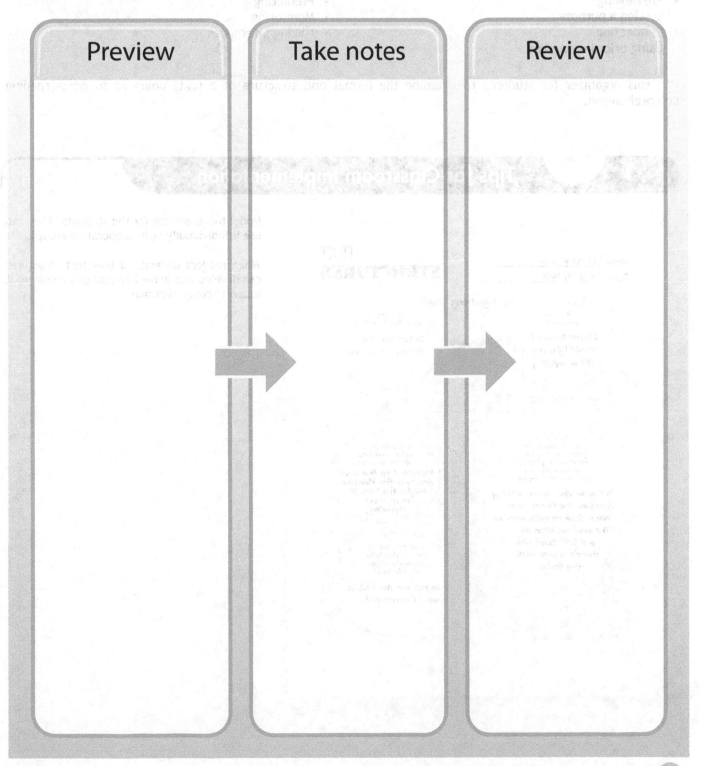

| Preview | Take notes | Review |

68   Text Structures

▶ Grades 5–12
▶ Social studies, English, science

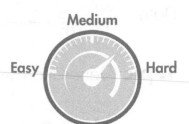

Students will develop the following reading strategies:

- Previewing
- Setting a purpose
- Connecting
- Using prior knowledge

- Predicting
- Monitoring
- Making inferences

Use this organizer for students to examine the format and structure of a text; doing so supports reading comprehension.

Tips for Classroom Implementation

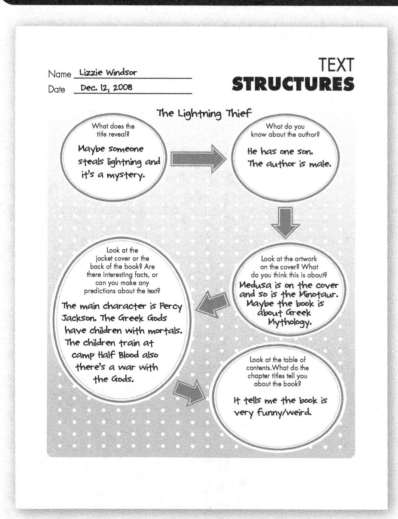

Model this organizer for the students. They can use it individually or in cooperative groups.

When readers understand how text structures can develop and impact an author's message, it supports comprehension.

Name _____

Date _____

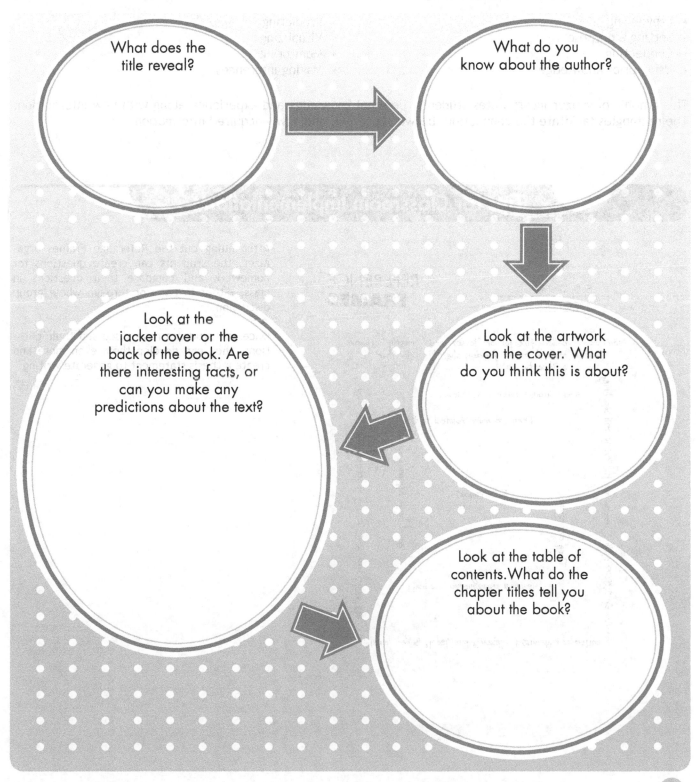

What does the title reveal?

What do you know about the author?

Look at the artwork on the cover. What do you think this is about?

Look at the jacket cover or the back of the book. Are there interesting facts, or can you make any predictions about the text?

Look at the table of contents. What do the chapter titles tell you about the book?

69 Reference Frames

▶ Grades 5–12
▶ Social studies, English, science

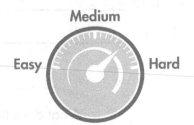

Medium

Easy ——————— Hard

Students will develop the following reading strategies:

- Previewing
- Setting a purpose
- Connecting
- Using prior knowledge

- Predicting
- Visualizing
- Monitoring
- Making inferences

This graphic organizer incorporates students' personal knowledge and experience along with new information. The rectangles facilitate the connections between previous and newly acquired information.

Tips for Classroom Implementation

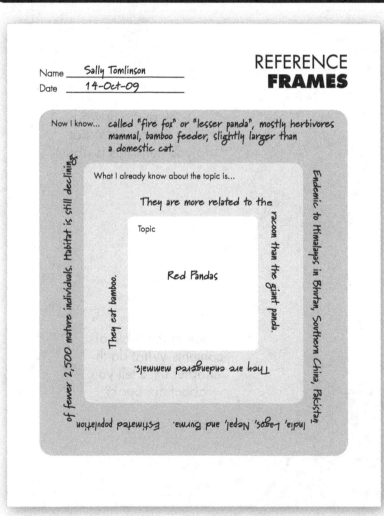

After filling out the Reference Frames organizer, the students can create questions for homework and compare their questions in class, either in pairs or through whole group discussion.

Once the students have discussed their questions, they can develop them even more and create a thesis statement to generate writing.

Name _____

Date _____

REFERENCE **FRAMES**

Now I know...

What I already know about the topic is...

Topic

70 Prior Knowledge

▶ Grades 5–12
▶ Social studies, English, science

Students will develop the following reading strategies:

- Previewing
- Setting a purpose
- Connecting
- Using prior knowledge
- Predicting

This graphic organizer prompts readers to think about that they already know about a topic and then apply it to the reading.

Tips for Classroom Implementation

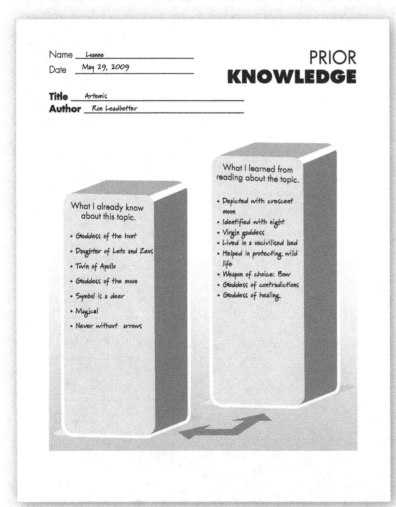

Name _Luanne_
Date _May 29, 2009_

PRIOR
KNOWLEDGE

Title _Artemis_
Author _Ron Leadbetter_

What I already know about this topic.

- Goddess of the hunt
- Daughter of Leto and Zeus
- Twin of Apollo
- Goddess of the moon
- Symbol is a deer
- Magical
- Never without arrows

What I learned from reading about the topic.

- Depicted with crescent moon
- Identified with night
- Virgin goddess
- Lived in a uncivilised land
- Helped in protecting wild life
- Weapon of choice: Bow
- Goddess of contradictions
- Goddess of healing

Remind students that they know about many different things and that this knowledge and information can help them with their reading. As a whole class, complete a sample graphic organizer as a model.

Name _____

Date _____

Title _____

Author _____

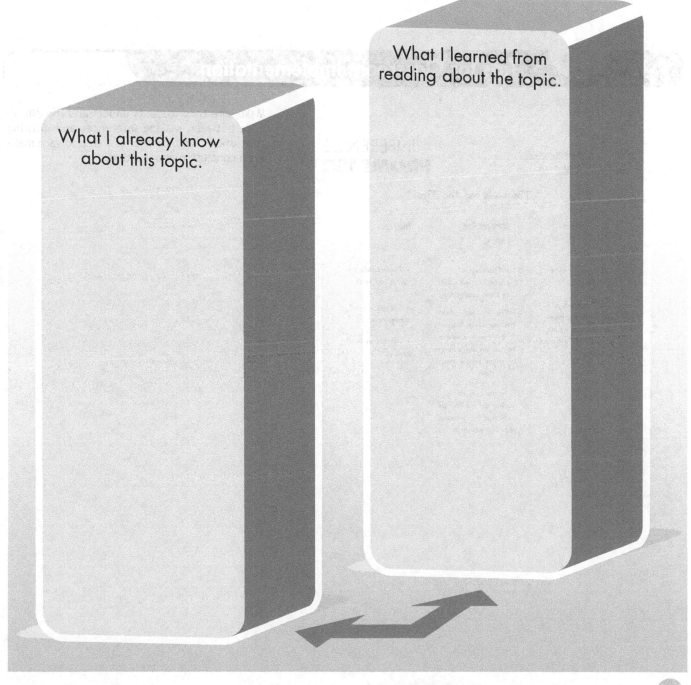

What I learned from reading about the topic.

What I already know about this topic.

71 Inference Prompter

▶ Grades 5—12
▶ Social studies, English, science

Medium

Easy ———— Hard

Students will develop the following reading strategies:

• Predicting
• Making inferences

Struggling readers usually have great difficulty in making inferences. Inferences are logical guesses that are based on what is not directly stated in a text.

Tips for Classroom Implementation

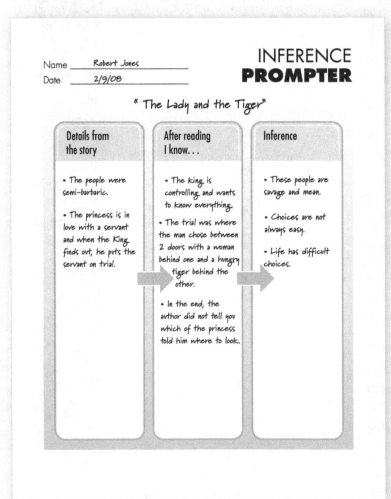

Make sure that students understand the difference between making inferences and drawing conclusions. An inference is a step toward making a conclusion about a text.

INFERENCE
PROMPTER

Name _____

Date _____

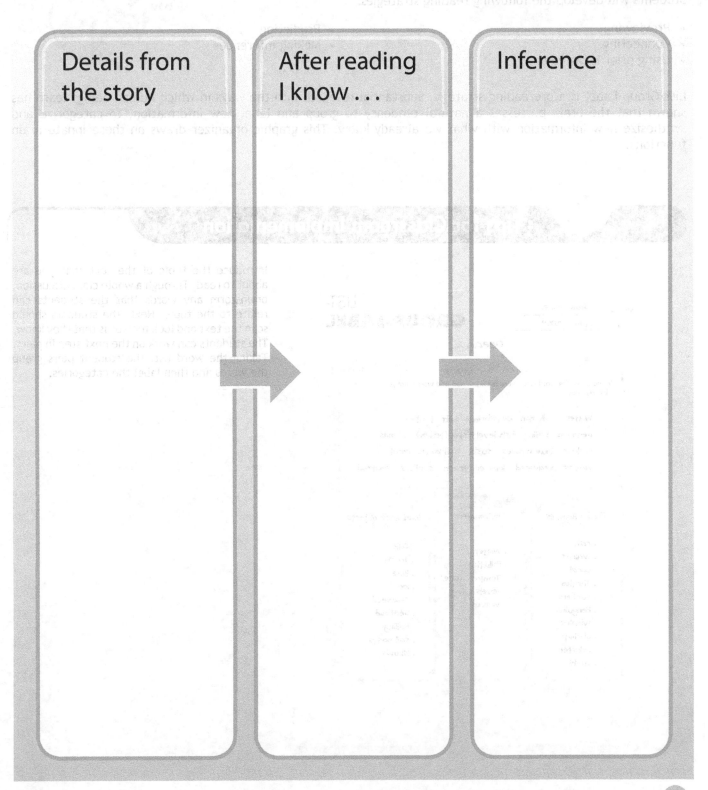

Details from the story	After reading I know . . .	Inference

72 List-Group-Label

▶ Grades 5—12
▶ Social studies, English, science, health

Students will develop the following reading strategies:

- Previewing
- Connecting
- Using prior knowledge

- Predicting
- Making inferences

List-Group-Label is a prereading strategy. Substantial research into the ways in which human beings learn has shown that the brain possesses a natural tendency to group and label new information, to categorize and synthesize new information with what we already know. This graphic organizer draws on these innate brain functions.

Tips for Classroom Implementation

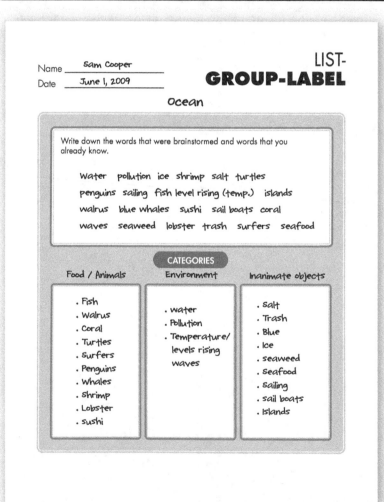

Name ___Sam Cooper___

Date ___June 1, 2009___

LIST-GROUP-LABEL

Ocean

Write down the words that were brainstormed and words that you already know.

Water   pollution ice shrimp salt turtles
penguins sailing fish level rising (temp.) islands
walrus blue whales sushi sail boats coral
waves seaweed lobster trash surfers seafood

CATEGORIES

Food / Animals
- Fish
- Walrus
- Coral
- Turtles
- Surfers
- Penguins
- Whales
- Shrimp
- Lobster
- sushi

Environment
- water
- Pollution
- Temperature/ levels rising waves

Inanimate objects
- Salt
- Trash
- Blue
- Ice
- seaweed
- Seafood
- Sailing
- sail boats
- Islands

Introduce the topic of the text that you are about to read. Through a whole class discussion, brainstorm any words that the students can relate to the topic. Next, the students should scan the text and look for words that they know. The students can work on the next step in pairs. Taking the word list, the student pairs group the words and then label the categories.

Name _____

Date _____

Write down the words that were brainstormed and words that you already know.

CATEGORIES

73 Think-Pair-Share

► Grades 5—12
► Social studies, English, science

Students will develop the following reading strategies:

- Previewing
- Setting a purpose
- Connecting
- Using prior knowledge

- Predicting
- Monitoring
- Making inferences

In this strategy, students will draw on their prior knowledge and share it with others. Active listening is also required. Structured discussion activities like Think-Pair-Share develop students' skills in being able to relate and discuss ideas.

Tips for Classroom Implementation

Pair the students and have each student recall all that he or she may already know about an assigned topic. As the students share information, encourage them to ask questions and ask for additional details. Students enjoy being able to share ideas and information as they are learning.

Name ___Darrius Foxgrover___
Date ___April 28, 2009___

THINK-PAIR-SHARE

TOPIC	Fractions
Partner 1 knows...	Partner 2 knows...
They can be top heavy or improper, numerator, denominator, two numbers that can be divided, translate into decimals and percents, part to part, are like ratios, are divided by a horizontal slash, they sometimes can be reduced. They can be multiplied, divided, added, or subtracted, part of math.	The numerator is the number above the line, the denominator is the number below the line. The line stands for division so $\frac{3}{4}$ is 3÷4. that is also how to find the decimal equivalent. Top-heavy fractions are when the numerator is of greater value than the denominator. Some fractions can be reduced. Mixed fractions are that number times the denominator.

THINK-
PAIR–SHARE

Name _____

Date _____

TOPIC	
Partner 1 knows. . .	Partner 2 knows. . .

74 The Five Ws

▶ Grades 5–12
▶ Social studies, English, science

Easy Medium Hard

Students will develop the following reading strategies:

- Connecting
- Using prior knowledge
- Predicting

- Monitoring
- Making inferences

Asking the five W questions is essential to any kind of inquiry. These are the five W questions:

1. What happened?
2. Who was there?
3. Why did it happen?

4. When did it happen?
5. Where did it happen?

These questions prompt students to explore the different elements of their reading. Through these questions, students will be able to identify the character and plot elements that will lead them to determine the author's major themes and ideas.

Tips for Classroom Implementation

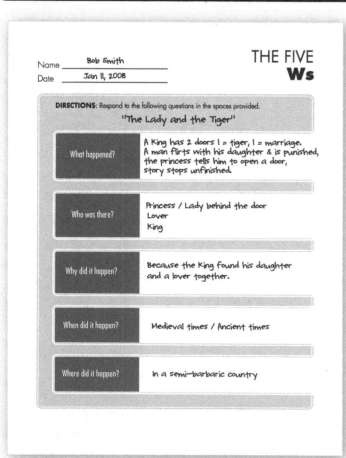

Name ____Bob Smith____
Date ____Jan 11, 2008____

THE FIVE
Ws

DIRECTIONS: Respond to the following questions in the spaces provided.

"The Lady and the Tiger"

What happened?
A King has 2 doors 1 = tiger, 1 = marriage. A man flirts with his daughter & is punished, the princess tells him to open a door, story stops unfinished.

Who was there?
Princess / Lady behind the door
Lover
King

Why did it happen?
Because the King found his daughter and a lover together.

When did it happen?
Medieval times / Ancient times

Where did it happen?
In a semi-barbaric country

Model how to answer the five W questions through a read-aloud with the students. This graphic organizer can be used by students individually, in pairs, or in groups.

Name _____

Date _____

DIRECTIONS: Respond to the following questions in the spaces provided.

What happened?

Who was there?

Why did it happen?

When did it happen?

Where did it happen?

Name

Date

DIRECTIONS: Respond to the following questions in the spaces provided.

CHAPTER SIX

Graphic Organizers for Writing

75 Autobiographical Poem

▶ Grades 5—12
▶ All subjects

This kind of writing is usually assigned at the beginning of the school year as a way for the students and teacher to get to know each other.

 Tips for Classroom Implementation

Model the autobiographical poem for your students. Write your responses and create a poem using the graphic organizer. Students enjoy sharing these poems, and you may want to create a classroom book of the students' autobiographical poems.

Name ___Ellie McKnight___
Date ___2/2/09___

AUTOBIOGRAPHICAL POEM

AUTOBIOGRAPHICAL POEM

DIRECTIONS: Write your responses and create a poem using this organizer.

Line 1	Your first name	Ellie
Line 2	Four adjectives that describe you	eccentric, creative, funny
Line 3	Resident of...	Chicago, IL
Line 4	Son or daughter of...	Katie and Jim
Line 5	Brother or sister of...	Colin
Line 6	Lover of... (3 terms)	theater, books, learning
Line 7	Who likes to... (2 items)	have fun, act
Line 8	Who hates to... (2 things)	play sports, fight with friends
Line 9	Who would like to... (3 things)	become an actress, athlete, or teacher
Line 10	Your last name	McKnight

Ellie
Eccentric, creative, funny
Resident of Chicago
Daughter of Katie and Jim
Sister of Colin
Lover of theater, books, and learning
Who likes to have fun and act
Who hates to play sports and fight with friends
Who would like to be an actress, athlete, or teacher
McKnight

Name _____

Date _____

AUTOBIOGRAPHICAL POEM

AUTOBIOGRAPHICAL POEM

DIRECTIONS: Write your responses and create a poem using this organizer.

Line 1	Your first name	
Line 2	Four adjectives that describe you	
Line 3	Resident of ...	
Line 4	Son or daughter of ...	
Line 5	Brother or sister of ...	
Line 6	Lover of ... (3 terms)	
Line 7	Who likes to ... (2 items)	
Line 8	Who hates to ... (2 things)	
Line 9	Who would like to ... (3 things)	
Line 10	Your last name	

76 Historical Bio Poem

▶ Grades 5–12
▶ All subjects

This biographical poem is adapted to include facts and concepts that focus on particular people, subjects, places, or events in all content areas.

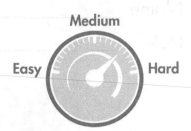

Easy — Medium — Hard

Tips for Classroom Implementation

Model the bio poem for the students. Students can create their bio poems individually or in groups.

Name **Bob Franklin**
Date **3/13/09**

HISTORICAL BIO POEM

DIRECTIONS: Write your responses and create a poem using this organizer.

Line 1	First name of subject	Benjamin Franklin
Line 2	Four adjectives that describe the subject	smart, persuasive, wise, and inventive
Line 3	Resident of...	Philadelphia, Pennsylvania
Line 4	Lover of... (3 people, places, or things)	America, science, writing
Line 5	Who believed...	that the states should be free
Line 6	Who used... (3 methods or things)	persuasion, science, and writing
Line 7	Who wanted... (3 things)	a strong, independent, and free nation.
Line 8	Who said... (give a quote)	"fish and guests are similar. They begin to smell after 3 days"

Benjamin Franklin
smart, persuasive, wise, and inventive
Resident of Philadelphia
Lover of America, science, writing
Who believed the states should be free
Who used persuasion, science, and writing
Who wanted a strong, independent, and free nation
Who said, "Fish and guests are similar.
They both begin to smell after three days."

Name _____

Date _____

HISTORICAL BIO POEM

HISTORICAL BIO POEM

DIRECTIONS: Write your responses and create a poem using this organizer.

Line 1	First name of subject	
Line 2	Four adjectives that describe the subject	
Line 3	Resident of...	
Line 4	Lover of... (3 people, places, or things)	
Line 5	Who believed...	
Line 6	Who used... (3 methods or things)	
Line 7	Who wanted... (3 things)	
Line 8	Who said... (give a quote)	

77 Inquiry Chart

▶ Grades 5—12
▶ Social studies, English, science, health, and science

An inquiry chart prompts students to record what they already know about a particular topic.

Easy ← → Medium / Hard

Tips for Classroom Implementation

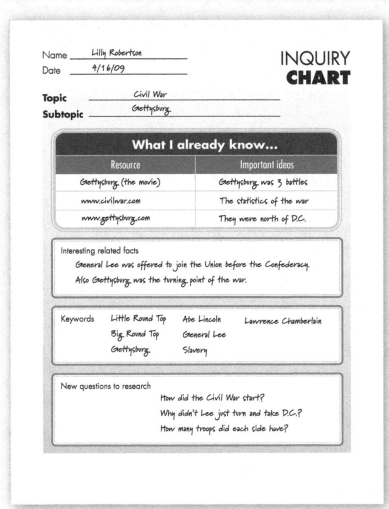

Name _____ Lilly Robertson _____
Date _____ 4/16/09 _____

INQUIRY CHART

Topic _____ Civil War _____
Subtopic _____ Gettysburg _____

What I already know...

Resource	Important ideas
Gettysburg (the movie)	Gettysburg was 3 battles
www.civilwar.com	The statistics of the war
www.gettysburg.com	They were north of D.C.

Interesting related facts
General Lee was offered to join the Union before the Confederacy.
Also Gettysburg was the turning point of the war.

Keywords   Little Round Top   Abe Lincoln   Lawrence Chamberlain
           Big Round Top   General Lee
           Gettysburg   Slavery

New questions to research
How did the Civil War start?
Why didn't Lee just turn and take D.C.?
How many troops did each side have?

Inquiry charts can be used individually, in small cooperative learning groups, or with the whole class. Students list their topic and any information that they already know about the topic. Next, they consult resources and note bibliographical information.

The limited amount of note-taking space is deliberate. It encourages students to selectively summarize important information. There is space on the organizer to record key words and questions that students might have while conducting their research.

Name _____

Date _____

INQUIRY
CHART

Topic _____

Subtopic _____

What I already know...

Resource	Important ideas

Interesting related facts

Key words

New questions to research

78 | Peer Review

► Grades 5–12
► Social studies, English, science, health, and science

Peer collaboration is an important part of today's classroom, and it plays a role in the teaching of writing. Exchanging writing drafts helps students develop their ideas and gain important peer feedback. When students are required to offer peer feedback, they often have a difficult time structuring their comments; this graphic organizer supplies that structure.

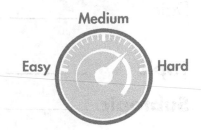

Tips for Classroom Implementation

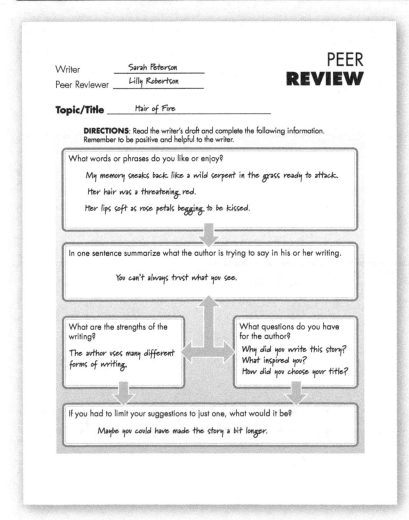

Writer _____ Sarah Peterson _____

Peer Reviewer _____ Lilly Robertson _____

PEER REVIEW

Topic/Title _____ Hair of Fire _____

DIRECTIONS: Read the writer's draft and complete the following information. Remember to be positive and helpful to the writer.

What words or phrases do you like or enjoy?

My memory sneaks back like a wild serpent in the grass ready to attack.

Her hair was a threatening red.

Her lips soft as rose petals begging to be kissed.

In one sentence summarize what the author is trying to say in his or her writing.

You can't always trust what you see.

What are the strengths of the writing?

The author uses many different forms of writing.

What questions do you have for the author?

Why did you write this story? What inspired you? How did you choose your title?

If you had to limit your suggestions to just one, what would it be?

Maybe you could have made the story a bit longer.

Here are two additional suggestions when using the Peer Review organizer:

- Remind the students to *be positive* about the writing that they are evaluating.
- Students should write comments and suggestions that will be helpful when the writer composes a subsequent draft.

Writer _____

Peer Reviewer _____

Topic/Title _____

DIRECTIONS: Read the writer's draft and complete the following information. Remember to be positive and helpful to the writer.

What words or phrases do you like or enjoy?

In one sentence summarize what the author is trying to say in his or her writing.

What are the strengths of the writing?

What questions do you have for the author?

If you had to limit your suggestions to just one, what would it be?

79 Entrance Slip

► Grades 5–12
► All subjects

This graphic organizer prompts students to tap into their prior knowledge and serves as an introduction to a new unit or topic. Entrance slips are one of the most frequently used content literacy strategies because they are so adaptable. They are effective tools for previewing content at the beginning of a class period. This activity helps students focus on the topic of the lesson and what they will be learning.

Easy — Hard

 Tips for Classroom Implementation

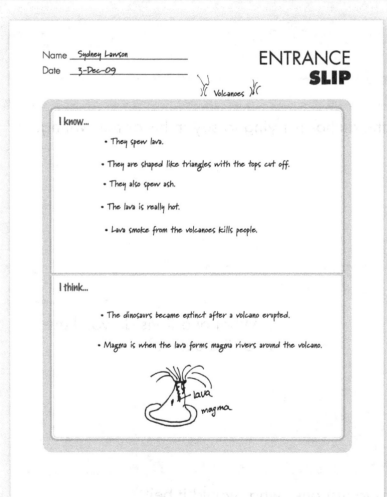

Distribute the entrance slip at the beginning of class and give students about three minutes to record their responses.

Name _____

Date _____

I know...

I think...

80 Exit Slip

▶ Grades 5–12
▶ All subjects

This graphic organizer prompts students to think about what they have learned. When students think about their learning, it is more likely to become part of their long-term memory and personal knowledge.

Easy   Hard

Tips for Classroom Implementation

Name _Olivia Doe_

Date _15-Mar-09_

EXIT SLIP

What did you learn today and why is it important?

Today I learned how volcanic islands were formed. They are formed when the volcano explodes. The lava cools on the water and hardens to form an island.

This is important because I have a better understanding of how some islands are made and world geology.

For a closure activity, distribute the exit slips and instruct students to think about what they have learned and why it is important. Exit slips are one of the most commonly used content literacy strategies and are an effective means of assessment. Many teachers use exit slips to determine how well students understand course content. Exit slips also make students account-able for what they have learned.

Name _____

Date _____

What did you learn today and why is it important?

81 Writer Checklist

▶ Grades 5—12
▶ All subjects

Easy   Hard

Prior to an individual teacher conference, the students should complete a checklist that guides them through the writing of their drafts. This writer checklist also fosters student independence and responsibility. Model the use of the checklist as needed.

Tips for Classroom Implementation

Name ___Bob Hughs___

Date ___12/2/09___

WRITER CHECKLIST

WRITER CHECKLIST		
Title of piece Hair of Fire		
	Yes	No
I have solid paragraphs that contain a main idea.	✓	
Grammar is correct.	✓	
Punctuation is correct.	✓	
I have periods at the end of each sentence.	✓	
I have quotation marks to indicate dialogue.	✓	
My spelling is correct.	✓	
I have sentence variety.	✓	
My sentences make sense.	✓	
I used transitions.		✓
My sentences are complete.	✓	
There are no run-ons.	✓	
There are no sentence fragments.	✓	
I have an introduction that draws the reader in to my writing.	✓	
I have correctly capitalized titles.	✓	
My ideas are written in my own words.	✓	
I have details that help the reader to understand my topic.	✓	
My ideas and information are related to each other.		✓
I have listened to feedback from my teacher and peers on earlier drafts and applied it to my final draft.		✓

When students reflect on their individual work, they are more likely to retain what they have learned. In countless instances, I have distributed the Writer Checklist to students when they claim that they are "ready to submit" the draft. I hand them the checklist and the student will often say, "I need to go back and revise some more" when they see that they have not met all of the expectations on the Writer's Checklist. It is more valuable when students can critically examine their own work and make corrections and revisions as needed.

Name _____

Date _____

WRITER CHECKLIST

Title of piece		Yes	No
I have solid paragraphs that contain a main idea.			
Grammar is correct.			
Punctuation is correct.			
I have periods at the end of each sentence.			
I have quotation marks to indicate dialogue.			
My spelling is correct.			
I have sentence variety.			
My sentences make sense.			
I used transitions.			
My sentences are complete.			
There are no run-ons.			
There are no sentence fragments.			
I have an introduction that draws the reader in to my writing.			
I have correctly capitalized titles.			
My ideas are written in my own words.			
I have details that help the reader to understand my topic.			
My ideas and information are related to each other.			
I have listened to feedback from my teacher and peers on earlier drafts and applied it to my final draft.			

82 Sensory Starter

▶ Grades 5—12
▶ All subjects

Good writers use rich sensory details that facilitate the reader's ability to visualize the events in a text. This graphic organizer prompts students to compile sensory details as a prewriting activity. Model for the students how to use this graphic organizer as a prewriting tool.

Tips for Classroom Implementation

Name _____Charlie_____
Date _____March 30_____

SENSORY STARTER

Topic	Medieval Peasants			
See	**Touch**	**Smell**	**Taste**	**Hear**
Crops	Rough dirt	Sweet flowers	Awful	Birds
Cattle	Slippery	Stinky dirt	Sweet	Calling
Porridge	Soft beds		Bitter	Crying
Dung	Rough walls	Bitter food	Salty	Loud
Sky				Quiet
Trees				Busy
Houses				Talking
				Grunting

As a prewriting tool, the Sensory Starter prompts students to record details that can enhance a student's writing. When I give students a prompt, I will always have at least one students who claims, "I can't think of anything." The Sensory Starter can provide support for a student to cobble details and being to visualize what they will write about. If students can "see" and picture what they will write about, it facilitates the drafting process. Sensory details are especially important for student writers because they help the reader to "see" what the writer "sees".

Name _____

Date _____

SENSORY STARTER

Topic				
See	Touch	Smell	Taste	Hear

83 Story Map I

▶ Grades 5—12
▶ All subjects

Understanding the elements of a good story is critical for student writers. This graphic organizer reminds students of the essential elements of story structure. Model how to use this prewriting graphic organizer during whole group instruction.

Easy   Hard

 Tips for Classroom Implementation

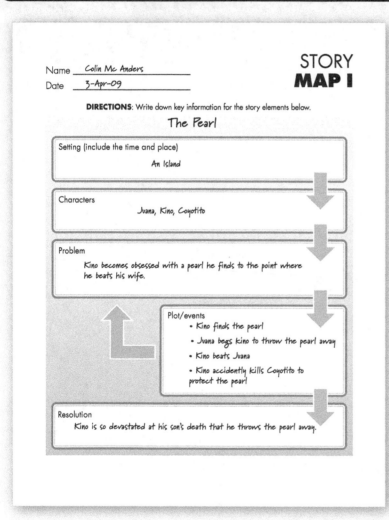

Name Colin Mc Anders

Date 3-Apr-09

STORY
MAP I

DIRECTIONS: Write down key information for the story elements below.

The Pearl

Setting (include the time and place)
An Island

Characters
Juana, Kino, Coyotito

Problem
Kino becomes obsessed with a pearl he finds to the point where he beats his wife.

Plot/events
• Kino finds the pearl
• Juana begs Kino to throw the pearl away
• Kino beats Juana
• Kino accidentally kills Coyotito to protect the pearl

Resolution
Kino is so devastated at his son's death that he throws the pearl away.

Howard Gardner was one of the pioneers in identifying the needs of different kinds of learners. Essentially, the more modalities we integrate in our lessons, the more likely our students will internalize new information and skills. The Story Map facilitates the students' organization, analysis, and understanding of a story. In other words, it helps students to keep the information straight. The kind of information that is used to complete a story map is often conveyed by the teacher in a large group discussion. Imagine how difficult this might be for student who has some difficulty in processing information orally. Before the story is discussed in a large group discussion, have the students work individually or in pairs to complete the Story Map. This should only take 5-7 minutes and then conduct a large group discussion. Most likely, more students will participate and there will be greater depth to the large group discussion. Once the students have mastered Story Map I, they are ready for the more complex Story Map II.

Name _____

Date _____

DIRECTIONS: Write down key information for the story elements below.

Setting (include the time and place)

Characters

Problem

Plot/events

Resolution

84 Story Map II

► Grades 5–12
► All subjects

This is a somewhat more detailed version of Story Map I. Model how to use this prewriting graphic organizer during whole group instruction.

Easy — Hard

Tips for Classroom Implementation

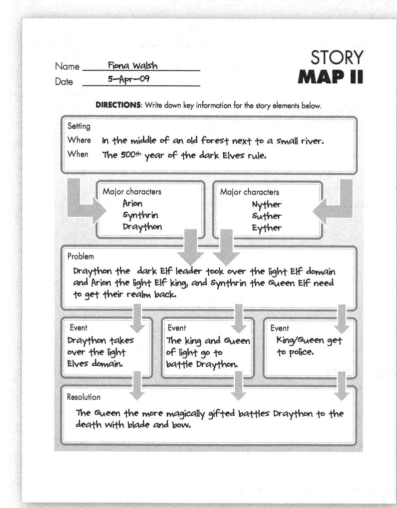

Name ___Fiona Walsh___
Date ___5–Apr–09___

STORY MAP II

DIRECTIONS: Write down key information for the story elements below.

Setting
Where   In the middle of an old forest next to a small river.
When   The 500th year of the dark Elves rule.

Major characters
Arion
Synthrin
Draython

Major characters
Nyther
Suther
Eyther

Problem
Draython the dark Elf leader took over the light Elf domain and Arion the light Elf king, and Synthrin the Queen Elf need to get their realm back.

Event
Draython takes over the light Elves domain.

Event
The king and Queen of light go to battle Draython.

Event
King/Queen get to police.

Resolution
The Queen the more magically gifted battles Draython to the death with blade and bow.

(See comments for Graphic Organizer 83)

Once the students have mastered Story Map I (graphic organizer 83) they are ready for this more complex version. This version requires the students to be more detailed in their analysis of the text. Characters and major events must be identified and related to the major plot points. The students can visualize how the events and characters are related in this visual representation. When I use Story Maps, I remind the students that they can always make adjustments to the graphic organizers. For example, the students can use highlighters and different colors to connect information that is related to a particular character or event. I find it very helpful for the students to complete this graphic organizer in pairs prior to a large group discussion. It usually takes the students 7–10 minutes to complete this organizer.

Name _____

Date _____

DIRECTIONS: Write down key information for the story elements below.

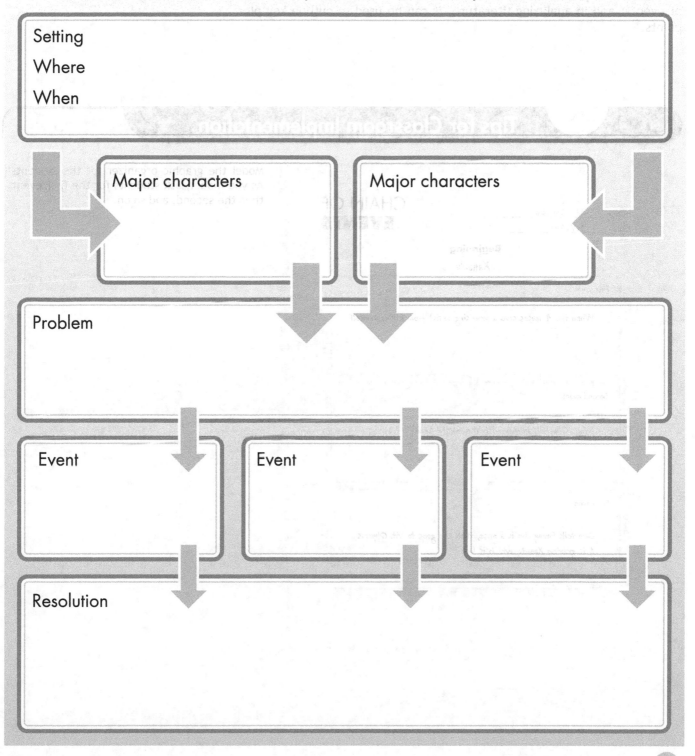

Setting
Where
When

Major characters

Major characters

Problem

Event

Event

Event

Resolution

85   Chain of Events

▶ Grades 5–12
▶ All subjects

The Chain of Events organizer is used to describe the actions of a character or the stages of events. In a science class, it is useful for organizing the elements of a phenomenon; in social studies, it can document a series of events; and in analyzing literature, it can be used to outline key plot points.

Easy   Hard

Tips for Classroom Implementation

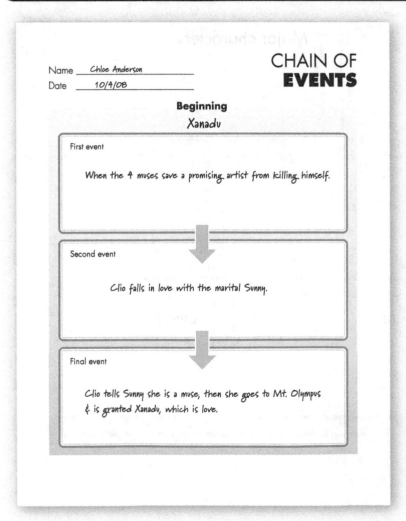

Name _Chloe Anderson_
Date _10/4/08_

CHAIN OF EVENTS

Beginning
Xanadu

First event

When the 4 muses save a promising artist from killing himself.

Second event

Clio falls in love with the marital Sunny.

Final event

Clio tells Sunny she is a muse, then she goes to Mt. Olympus & is granted Xanadu, which is love.

Model the graphic organizer for the students. As you model, ask students for the first event, then the second, and so on.

Name _____

Date _____

Beginning

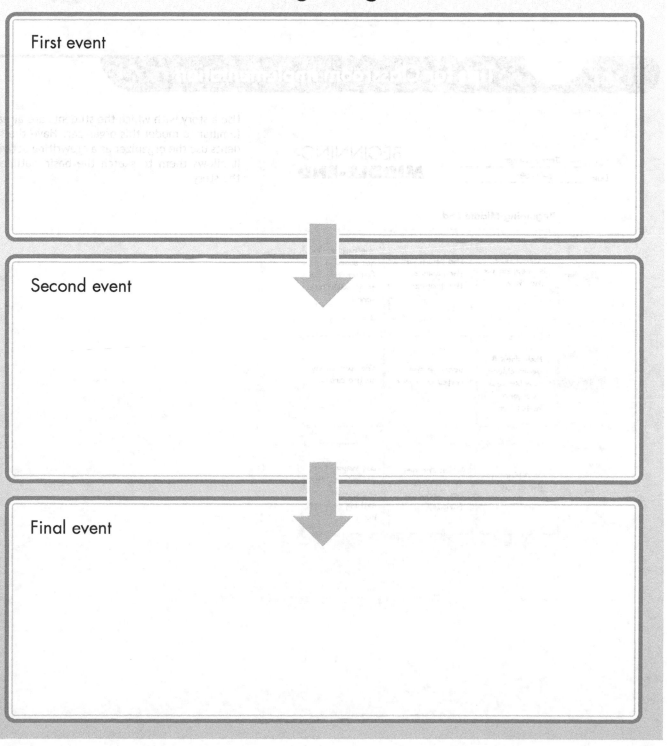

First event

Second event

Final event

86 Beginning-Middle-End

▶ Grades 5–12
▶ All subjects

This graphic organizer helps students organize story ideas and details into the fundamental story sequence of beginning, middle, and end.

Easy   Hard

Tips for Classroom Implementation

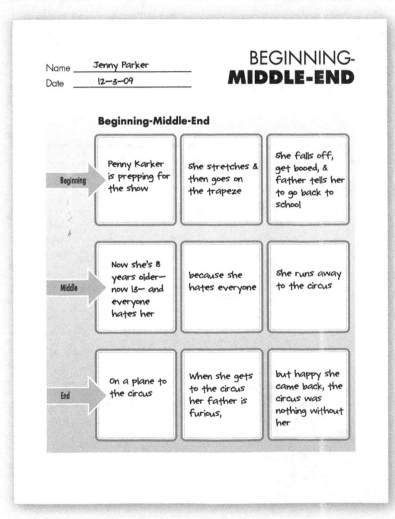

Name ___Jenny Parker___
Date ___12-3-09___

BEGINNING-MIDDLE-END

Beginning-Middle-End

Beginning
- Penny Karker is prepping for the show
- she stretches & then goes on the trapeze
- she falls off, get booed, & father tells her to go back to school

Middle
- Now she's 8 years older— now 13— and everyone hates her
- because she hates everyone
- she runs away to the circus

End
- On a plane to the circus
- When she gets to the circus her father is furious,
- but happy she came back, the circus was nothing without her

Use a story with which the students are already familiar to model this organizer. Have the students use the organizer as a prewriting activity. It allows them to sketch the basic outline of the story.

Name _____

Date _____

Beginning-Middle-End

Beginning

Middle

End

87 Climax Ladder

▶ Grades 5—12
▶ All subjects

Creating a chain of events that lead toward the climax of the story is challenging for a writer.

Easy   Hard

Tips for Classroom Implementation

Name _Elliot McDonald_
Date _4/4/09_

CLIMAX LADDER

A man goes to jail for life.

He finds a piece of paper with instructions to escape.

The prisoner decides to go in the escape tunnel.

The prisoner falls down the tunnel and can't turn back.

Use a story with which the students are already familiar to model this graphic organizer. As students are drafting their story, they can use the organizer to create a coherent string of events that will lead to an effective story climax.

Name _____

Date _____

CLIMAX
LADDER

88–91 Persuasive Writing Organizers

▶ Grades 5—12
▶ All subjects

Persuasive writing is most commonly assigned in the upper grades and high school. These tools help students organize their ideas into cogent arguments.

Tips for Classroom Implementation

Model the four different organizers during large group instruction.

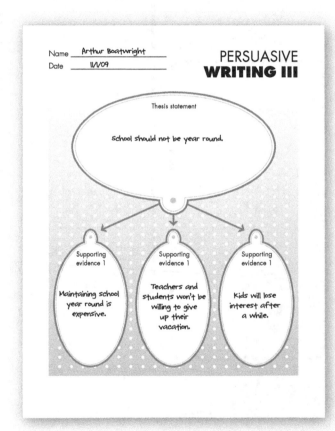

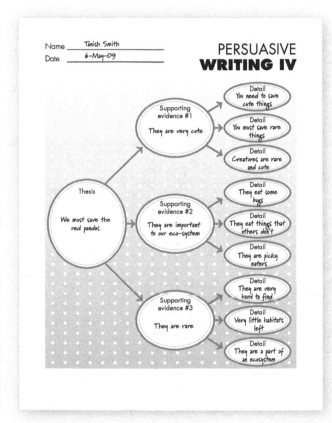

Name _____

Date _____

Topic _____

Opening sentences

Transition (word or phrase)

Support #1 topic sentence

Supporting evidence and details

Transition (word or phrase)

Support #2 topic sentence

Supporting evidence and details

Transition (word or phrase)

Support #3 topic sentence

Supporting evidence and details

Conclusion

PERSUASIVE
WRITING II

Topic _____

Introduction
Main idea thesis statement
Supporting evidence:
#1
#2
#3
Conclusion sentence

Evidence #1
Detail/Example 1
Detail/Example 2
Detail/Example 3
Concluding sentence

Evidence #2
Detail/Example 1
Detail/Example 2
Detail/Examplo 3
Concluding sentence

Evidence #3
Detail/Example 1
Detail/Example 2
Detail/Example 3
Concluding sentence

Concluding paragraph
Restate Main Idea:

Restate supporting reasons:

Recommendations and/or predictions:

Name _____

Date _____

PERSUASIVE
WRITING III

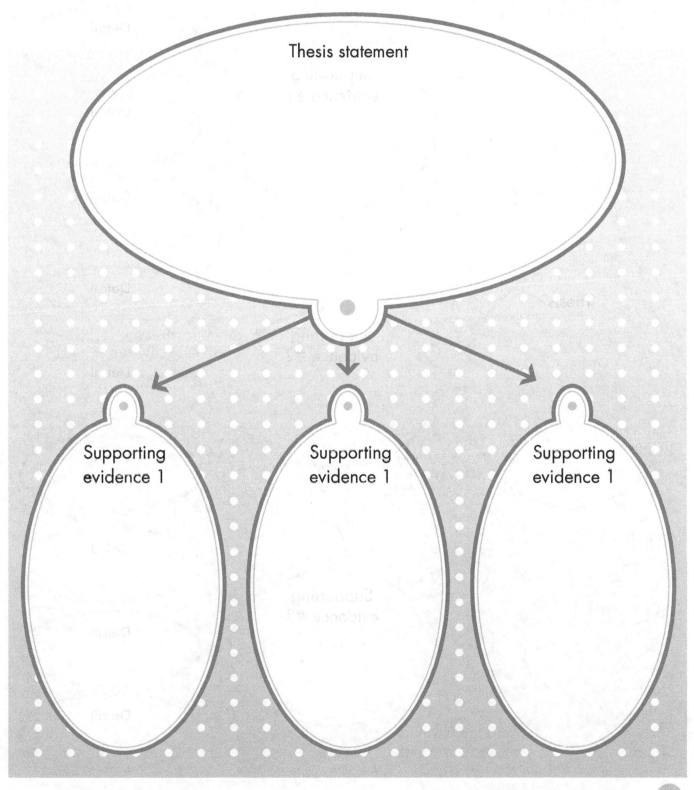

Thesis statement

Supporting evidence 1

Supporting evidence 1

Supporting evidence 1

Name _____

Date _____

PERSUASIVE
WRITING IV

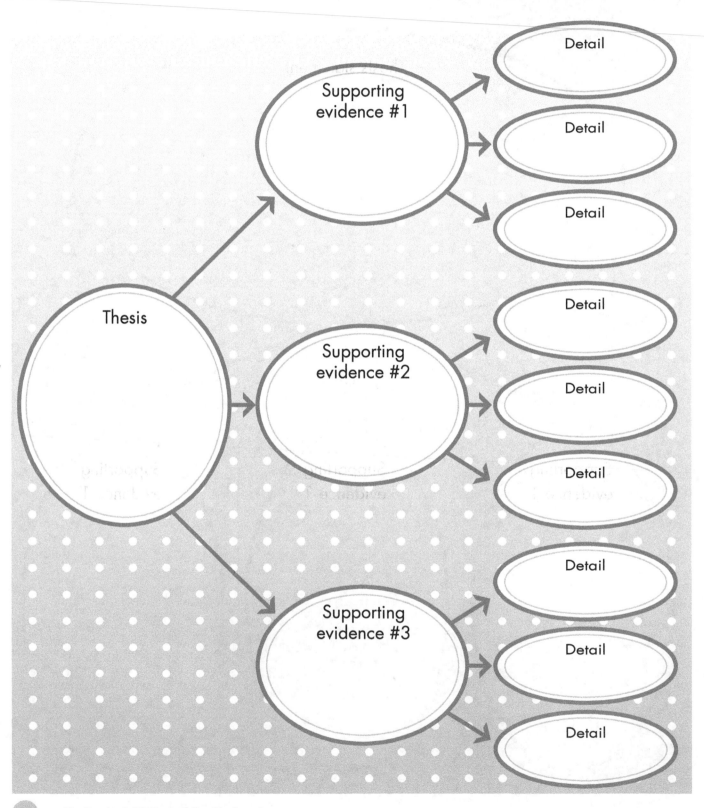

- Grades 5–12
- All subjects

This graphic organizer helps students compare a writing draft to an assessment rubric they have already received. Once they make this comparison, they have a plan for revision, with specific details and ideas. This organizer promotes students' independence in developing a systematic plan for revising their writing.

Tips for Classroom Implementation

Model how to use this graphic organizer. The students can work in pairs to analyze writing drafts.

92 Writing Revision Organizer

▶ Grades 5—12
▶ All subjects

This graphic organizer helps students compare a writing draft to an assessment rubric they have already received. Once they make this comparison, they have a plan for revision with specific details and ideas. This organizer promotes students' independence in developing a systematic plan for revising their writing.

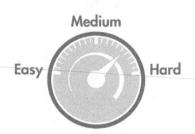

Tips for Classroom Implementation

Model how to use this graphic organizer. The students can work in pairs to analyze writing drafts.

Name _Wesley Karlon_
Date _1—Feb—09_

WRITING REVISION ORGANIZER

WRITING REVISION ORGANIZER

DIRECTIONS: Look at the rubric that you received for this writing assignment. Look at your writing draft and determine how your draft meets the rubric requirements and how it is different from the rubric requirements.

Science lab report: Pig dissection

	My writing is similar to the rubric	My writing is different from the rubric
Content	All of the pig parts were labeled as described	I have met this criteria.
Organization	I have organized the conclusion and results were organized in two ¶s.	I could've separated the results in three ¶s.
Spelling, grammar, punctuation	I spelled most words right.	I misspelled a few words.
Support and details	I described all of the pig parts.	I could've described them with more detail.

In my revision, I will. . .

Check all of the spelling and descriptive words.

Name _____

Date _____

WRITING REVISION ORGANIZER

DIRECTIONS: Look at the rubric that you received for this writing assignment. Look at your writing draft and determine how your draft meets the rubric requirements and how it is different from the rubric requirements.

	My writing is similar to the rubric	My writing is different from the rubric
Content		
Organization		
Spelling, grammar, punctuation		
Support and details		

In my revision, I will …

93 Prewriting Organizer

▶ Grades 5–12
▶ All subjects

This graphic organizer helps students determine the topic, audience, and purpose for a particular piece of writing.

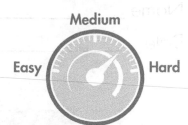

Easy — Medium — Hard

Tips for Classroom Implementation

PREWRITING
ORGANIZER

Name _____ Sarah Parker _____
Date _____ 20-Sep-09 _____

Elves/War

TOPIC	AUDIENCE	PURPOSE
What am I going to write about? What do I know about this topic? What information do I need to write about this topic? Where will I be able to find this information?	Who will read my writing? What could my audience already know about this topic? How could my writing influence what my audience thinks about the topic?	What reaction or response do I want my writing to prompt? What should this writing accomplish?
Elves and their war. I need to know about Elves' swords, bows/arrows, and magic. I know about Elves and bows/arrows. I can find this info in books and online.	My teachers and class. Almost nothing at all. By how they learn what they look like and how they act.	I want my writing to prompt questioning and understanding about magical beings.

The students, through whole class instruction, can complete the graphic organizer so that there are several models to which the students can refer. This is also a useful homework activity.

Name _____

Date _____

PREWRITING
ORGANIZER

TOPIC	AUDIENCE	PURPOSE
What am I going to write about? What do I know about this topic? What information do I need to write about this topic? Where will I be able to find this information?	Who will read my writing? What could my audience already know about this topic? How could my writing influence what my audience thinks about the topic?	What reaction or response do I want my writing to prompt? What should this writing accomplish?

94   What Happens?

▶ Grades 5—12
▶ All subjects

This graphic organizer supports students in outlining a narrative story.

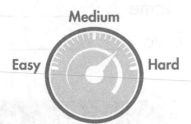

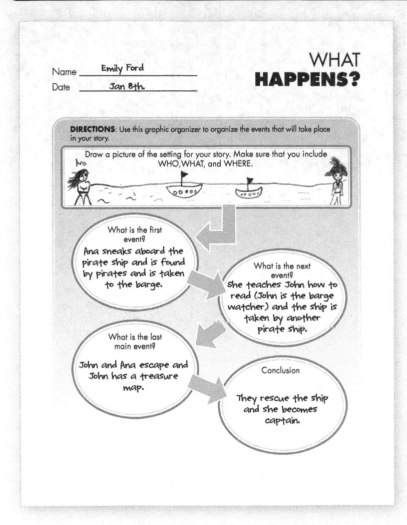

Model how to use this organizer; you might want to use a story that is the familiar to the students.

Name _____

Date _____

DIRECTIONS: Use this graphic organizer to organize the events that will take place in your story.

Draw a picture of the setting for your story. Make sure that you include WHO, WHAT, and WHERE.

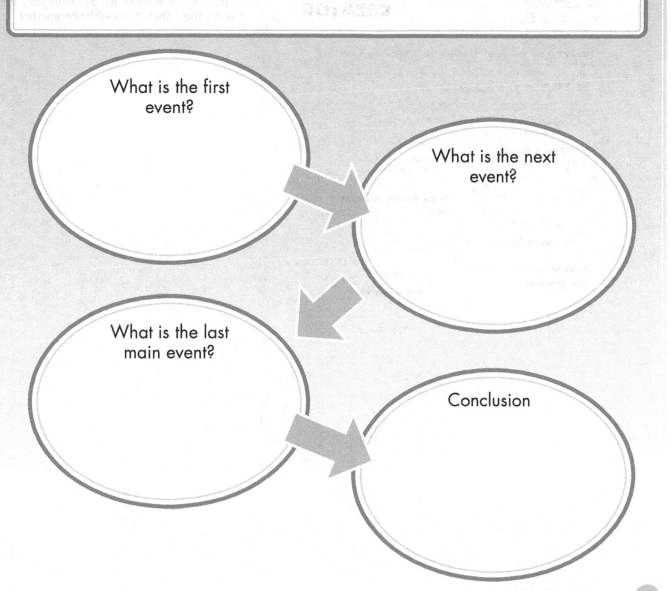

What is the first event?

What is the next event?

What is the last main event?

Conclusion

95 Character Creator

▶ Grades 5—12
▶ English

Students can use this graphic organizer to help them create a main character for a narrative story.

Medium
Easy — Hard

Tips for Classroom Implementation

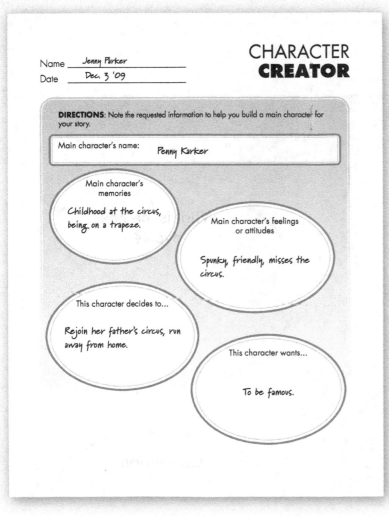

Name _Jenny Parker_
Date _Dec. 3 '09_

CHARACTER
CREATOR

DIRECTIONS: Note the requested information to help you build a main character for your story.

Main character's name: _Penny Karker_

Main character's memories
Childhood at the circus, being on a trapeze.

Main character's feelings or attitudes
Spunky, friendly, misses the circus.

This character decides to...
Rejoin her father's circus, run away from home.

This character wants...
To be famous.

Model how to use this graphic organizer for the students, perhaps using a character with whom they are familiar. The students can work in pairs or as individuals. Students also enjoy sharing their characters with one another.

Name _____

Date _____

CHARACTER
CREATOR

DIRECTIONS: Note the requested information to help you build a main character for your story.

Main character's name:

Main character's memories

Main character's feelings or attitudes

This character decides to...

This character wants...

96 Conflict and Solution Organizer

▶ Grades 5—12
▶ English

Every good piece of narrative writing has a conflict and a solution. This organizer reminds student writers of this important fundamental component of narrative writing.

Tips for Classroom Implementation

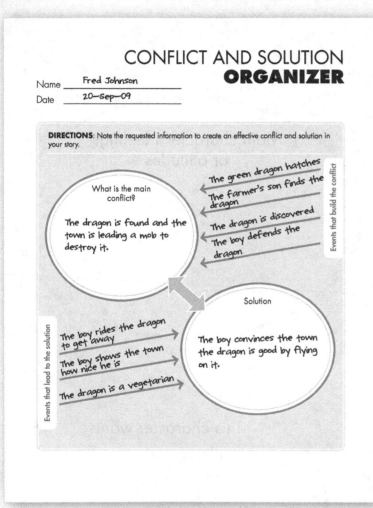

Model how to use this graphic organizer for the students. The students can work in pairs or as individuals.

CONFLICT AND SOLUTION
ORGANIZER

Name _____

Date _____

DIRECTIONS: Note the requested information to create an effective conflict and solution in your story.

What is the main conflict?

Events that build the conflict

Solution

Events that lead to the solution

97 Getting Ready to Write

▶ Grades 5–12
▶ English

This graphic organizer supports students during the prewriting stage of the writing process. Demonstrate how to use this graphic organizer through whole group discussion.

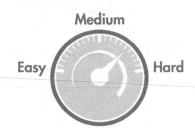

Easy   Medium   Hard

Tips for Classroom Implementation

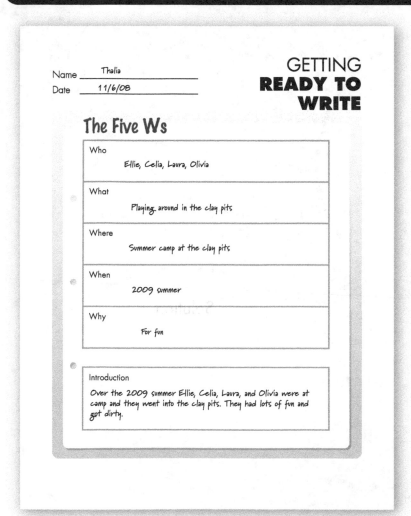

Name _____Thalia_____
Date _____11/6/08_____

GETTING READY TO WRITE

The Five Ws

Who
Ellie, Celia, Laura, Olivia

What
Playing around in the clay pits

Where
Summer camp at the clay pits

When
2009 summer

Why
For fun

Introduction
Over the 2009 summer Ellie, Celia, Laura, and Olivia were at camp and they went into the clay pits. They had lots of fun and got dirty.

I often tell students that the prewriting phase in the writing process is probably the most important. It is in this phase that the students must harvest their ideas and begin to commit them to paper. The Five W's are foundational for any journalist. This organizer prompts students to identify the Five Ws. It has been my experience that students are often stumbled by "Why" they are writing about this particular event. Once the student writer is able to identify the "why" it springboards them into writing because they have identified the purpose/importance of the story.

Name _____

Date _____

The Five Ws

Who	
What	
Where	
When	
Why	

Introduction	

98   Writing Process

▶ Grades 5–12
▶ All subjects

Students can use this graphic organizer either as a review of or introduction to the writing process.

Easy   Medium   Hard

Tips for Classroom Implementation

Name ___Maria Stratt___

Date ___5/4/09___

WRITING PROCESS

DIRECTIONS: Use this graphic organizer to document your progress through the writing process.

PUBLISHING
I typed my essay.

EDITING
I rewrote my essay with all corrected mistakes.

REVISING
I corrected all spelling mistakes, and I added some more details.

WRITING
I decided to write a pursuasive essay stating my opinion that "Athens was better than Sparta."

PREWRITING
I wrote my ideas down in a diagram and started writing down examples to support them.

For lack of a better term, this graphic organizer makes students accountable for their writing. As students document what they have accomplished in their writing at each stage of the writing process, they reflect on what they have done and consider next steps. This kind of focused reflection fosters ownership of a student's work since they must document what they have accomplished in their work.

Name _____

Date _____

WRITING
PROCESS

DIRECTIONS: Use this graphic organizer to document your progress through the writing process.

PUBLISHING

EDITING

REVISING

WRITING

PREWRITING

99 Story Pyramid

▶ Grades 5–12
▶ English

This graphic organizer helps students organize story components, which makes it a useful prewriting tool. Model it through whole-group instruction.

Easy — Medium — Hard

 Tips for Classroom Implementation

Name __Mary Brown__
Date __11/11/09__

STORY PYRAMID

DIRECTIONS: Write the requested information in the spaces below.

Susie Crow
Main character's name

Shallow   Pretty
Two words describing this person

Small   Quiet   Boring
Three words describing the setting or place

Cruel   Unexpected   Simple   Devastating
Four words describing an important event

Metamorphosis   Realization   Happy   Selflessness   Great
Five words describing the main idea or the importance of this event

---

Sometimes, documenting one's understanding with fewer words is far more challenging. When I ask students to summarize or identify their understanding with fewer words they often proclaim that they are "stuck". When I challenge them to go back and keep revising until their analysis is expressed exactly with the number of words requested, I notice that they are more precise and critical in the analysis. The Story Pyramid prompts students to precise and economical as possible in the character analysis.

Name _____

Date _____

STORY
PYRAMID

DIRECTIONS: Write the requested information in the spaces below.

Main character's name

Two words describing this person

Three words describing the setting or place

Four words describing an important event

Five words describing the main idea or the importance of this event

100 RAFT

▶ Grades 5–12
▶ All subjects

RAFT stands for *role, audience, format,* and *topic.* This organizer helps students plan successful writing.

Easy   Medium   Hard

Tips for Classroom Implementation

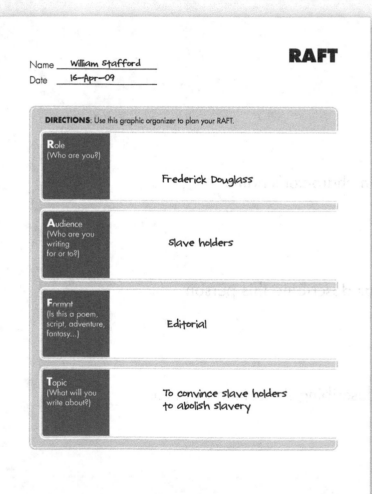

Name William Stafford
Date 16–Apr–09

RAFT

DIRECTIONS: Use this graphic organizer to plan your RAFT.

Role
(Who are you?)

Frederick Douglass

Audience
(Who are you writing for or to?)

Slave holders

Format
(Is this a poem, script, adventure, fantasy...)

Editorial

Topic
(What will you write about?)

To convince slave holders to abolish slavery

Explain each of the organizer elements.

Role. Students can take on any role they like, such as that of a scientist or a specific historical figure.
Audience. This could be another author, the U.S. Congress, or any real or imaginary group.
Format. Students can choose any format. Here are some suggestions:

Journal or diary	Play	Science fiction
Letter	Newspaper article	Fantasy
Job description	Editorial	Fairy tale
Resume	Advertisement	Adventure
Interview	Cartoon	Brochure
Science report	Travelogue	Children's book
Memo	Song	How-to book
Poem	Picture book	Television script

Topic. This could be one that you assign, or students can select one from assigned material.

Name _____

Date _____

DIRECTIONS: Use this graphic organizer to plan your RAFT.

Role
(Who are you?)

Audience
(Who are you writing for or to?)

Format
(Is this a poem, script, adventure, fantasy…)

Topic
(What will you write about?)

REFERENCES

Beck, I., McKeown, M., Hamilton, R., & Kucan, L. (1997). *Questioning the author: An approach for enhancing student engagement with text*. Newark, DE: International Reading Association.

Cassidy, J. (1991). Using graphic organizers to develop critical thinking. *Gifted Child Today, 12*(6), 34–36.

Gardner, H. (1993). *Frames of mind: The theory of multiple intelligences*. New York: Basic Books.

Gardner, H. (2006). *Multiple intelligences: New horizons in theory and practice*. New York: Basic Books.

Manzo, A., Manzo, V., & Estes, T. (2001). *Content area literacy: Interactive teaching for interactive learning* (2nd ed.). Hoboken, NJ: Wiley.

Materna, L. (2007). *Jump-start the adult learner: How to engage and motivate adults using brain-compatible strategies*. Thousand Oaks, CA: Corwin Press.

McKeown, M. G., Beck, I. L., & Worthy, M. J. (1993). Grappling with text ideas: Questioning the author. *Reading Teacher, 46*, 560–566.

Ogle, D. (1986). K-W-L: A teaching model that develops active reading of expository text. *Reading Teacher, 39*, 563–570.

Piaget, J. (1974). *The thought and language of the child* (M. Gabain, Trans.). New York: New American Library.

Raphael, T. (1982). Question-answering strategies for children. *Reading Teacher, 36*, 186–191.

Vygotsky, L. S. (1962). *Thought and language*. Cambridge, MA: MIT Press.